A Guide to Child Rearing

A Guide to Child Rearing

A Manual for Parents to Accompany

Help! I'm a Parent

Dr. Bruce Narramore
Psychologist

ZONDERVAN
PUBLISHING HOUSE OF THE ZONDERVAN CORPORATION
GRAND RAPIDS, MICHIGAN 49506

A GUIDE TO CHILD REARING

A Manual for Parents to Accompany
Help! I'm a Parent!

Copyright © 1972 by The Zondervan Corporation
Grand Rapids, Michigan

Ninth printing   February 1978
ISBN 0-310-30311-7

Library of Congress Catalog Card Number: 70 — 189584
Printed in the United States of America

CONTENTS

Chapter 1

PARENTS ARE MADE, NOT BORN

A story is told of Mr. Brown, a man who really loved the neighbor's children. He had a reputation for being kind to all the kids. One day Mr. Brown poured a new cement driveway. After dark some mischievous children found the fresh cement. They placed their footprints in the drive and left a few initials. The next morning when he discovered the results, Mr. Brown blew his stack. He was red with anger! He shouted threats throughout the block and couldn't wait to get his hands on the culprits!

Mr. Brown's neighbors were surprised by this sudden outburst. It seemed so out of character for a man who loved the village children. Finally someone got up nerve to ask about his outburst. The neighbor said, "I thought you loved all children. Why are you suddenly so angry?" Mr. Brown thought awhile and then replied, "I love them in the abstract, but not in the concrete!"

The moral of this story can apply to books on rearing children. It is one thing to read some abstract theory. It is another matter to make some concrete applications. This manual is designed to help you in the concrete. Effective child rearing takes some careful planning. It also requires a lot of practice. The exercises in this book can give you both. They will help review the main ideas of *Help! I'm a Parent!* and lead you to a deeper understanding of your child. They will also help you learn a step-by-step way of changing your child's behavior.

As a psychologist, I have gone through several phases. As a young graduate student counseling adolescents, I saw how most of their problems stemmed from faulty home relations. Soon I started blaming parents for every problem. If they would just shape up, their children would be okay.

A few years later I married and had my own children. Suddenly my reasoning changed. "Parents do the best they can," I told myself. "They can't be blamed when children run astray!" But this attitude didn't last long. As I honestly reviewed the situation, I had to admit that most of my children's misbehaviors could be traced to my own negative reactions. This is the only accurate perception. Proverbs 22:6 says, "Train up a child in the way he should go: and when he is old, he will not depart from it." This verse is very clear. If we train children properly, they will not go astray! Conversely, if we fail to raise them properly, we can expect continual problems. The experience of psychologists validates this text. Children with proper parental discipline do not develop serious problems. No matter how "good" a home may seem to an outsider, if children are having problems, the parents are to blame.[1]

By blame I don't mean we should condemn ourselves for each parental error. We are all in a process of growth that continues until we die. We should accept our humanness and our many errors. To condemn ourselves only makes matters worse. If we start feeling like a failure, we become depressed. This depression may result in increased frustration and further impair our relations with our children. The purpose of seeing our responsibility for our children's misbehavior is not to condemn ourselves for past failures. The object is to see the tremendous future opportunities to guide our sons and daughters into healthy adult adjustment. A key to that is the knowledge that we are the primary determinants of our children's life adjustment.

I hope these thoughts communicate one of the most important ideas you can ever learn. That is the absolute primacy of our responsibilities as parents. God has placed our children's physical, spiritual, and emotional destinies in our hands. One of the tragedies of life is that many of us are unwilling to put five percent of the amount of

---

[1]There are, of course, physical ailments such as glandular disturbances and neurological impairments which hamper the adjustment for some children. Even in these cases, however, things can be improved through proper methods of child training.

time we spend at work into learning to rear our children. If we will spend one or two hours of study weekly for a short time we can radically improve our relations with our children. *My strong desire for you is that you will be willing to take time to be a better parent!*

A PROGRAM FOR CHANGE

For the past several years I have spent much of my time counseling parents and lecturing on principles for raising children. In these situations I ran across many problems and shared a number of biblical and psychological insights with concerned parents. Before long, however, a frustration began to set in. Although I knew the child's problems and offered some solutions, many parents failed to carry through. It soon became obvious that knowledge wasn't enough. To become effective parents, most people needed training. But what kind of training? Parents couldn't be sent to school to learn effective ways of discipline. Most families couldn't afford long term counseling. And reading books and hearing a few lectures wasn't enough to bring lasting changes. Out of this frustration my wife and I began conducting seminars for parents. We combined accepted biblical and psychological principles with a specific plan for change. We developed a series of exercises which helped parents apply these principles to practical family problems. Almost immediately we sensed a difference. As parents took an hour or so a week to apply these principles, things began to happen. Parents reported a decrease in temper tantrums, solutions to sibling conflicts, improved school achievement, and a host of other changes.

The secret of these changes lies in this book. Parents were learning to *do* rather than to *think*. By completing the exercises, they were turning the abstract into concrete. As you work through the pages of this book, keep this principle in mind. No insight is really useful until it is thought through and put into action. That is hard for most of us to do. Reading a book and gaining new understanding is fun. But a careful and objective evaluation of our reactions to our children may be painful. We all like to think we are "good" parents. We love our children and are "trying our best." But we also tend to think that however we deal with children is the "proper" way. When we begin evaluating our parent-child relations critically, we can become discouraged. The easy thing to do is to forget the professional guidelines and keep on "doing what comes naturally." But in doing this, we make a grave mistake. We avoid the temporary frustrations of facing the inadequacy of our present methods. But we continue to suffer our daily family conflicts. When things go wrong, we blame our children or say, "That's normal for a child his age." As a psychologist and parent, I still find it difficult to admit I'm doing wrong with children. But I have also found this: when I do put out a little effort to apply a new technique I am rewarded many times over. There is a new reign of peace and the knowledge that I am giving my children a happy childhood and preparing them for a fulfilling life ahead.

To really learn new methods of coping with our children, we need three things. We need an effective plan for rearing children, a personal commitment to become a better parent, and a method to see that we carry out our program for growth. This book and *Help! I'm a Parent!* give important insights for raising children. Your reading of these books shows a commitment on your part to change. The only other ingredient is a method to carry out your study. Let me make the following suggestions. You should never do these exercises by yourself. Get one or more friends to join you. Then make a commitment to telephone each other at least once a week to see that you have completed that week's work. I suggest that you do one workbook chapter every week or two. If you go much faster, you will not have time to study your child's behavior carefully and apply your new insights. A longer period for each lesson is fine, provided you are still checking up on your study partner weekly to see that you are properly applying the principles.

HOW TO STUDY CHILD BEHAVIOR

When our daughter was eight or ten months old, she started throwing silverware on the floor. At nearly every meal, at least one spoon wound up on the floor. We tried to reason with her, but that didn't seem to help. We spanked her, but that didn't work either. We could have told her, "When you throw your spoon on the floor, that means you are finished eating until the next meal." With an older child that would have worked. But Debbie wasn't quite old enough to understand the logical consequence of having her food removed each time she threw a piece of silverware. We decided we would utilize spankings to cure the problem. We would tell her, "No, no," the next time she started to throw her spoon. Each time after that we would repeat the "no, no" and spank her hands lovingly, but firmly.

To see how effective our method worked, we decided to make a graph of her behavior. We didn't start our discipline for a few days;

so we could tell just how bad the problem was. The chart below graphs Debbie's spoon-throwing behavior. Discipline started on day five. Notice what happened. There was no change the first day. Since we had inconsistently spanked her before, she didn't realize we meant business this time. On day six (the second day of our plan) she still threw three spoons on the floor, an average of one per meal. By day seven (the third day of "operation spoon") we were really getting results. On day eight the negative behavior disappeared. We thought we had the problem licked. But Debbie had another thought. She wanted to be sure we would be consistent. So on day nine she gave it one more try. When she was spanked again, she was finally satisfied. She had learned it *never* paid to throw a spoon on the floor.

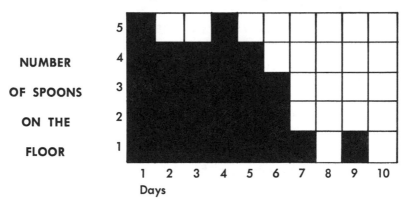

NUMBER OF SPOONS ON THE FLOOR

Days

A chart like this is a good tool in changing your child's behavior. By plotting a misbehavior for a few days, we give a foundation for future change. We know objectively just how frequently a problem recurs. When we begin to apply a method of discipline, a chart tells us our success. We don't need to say, "I think he's doing better." We can study the graph and see the results for ourselves.

A graph of misbehavior also serves another important function. It forces us to plan a program for behavior change carefully and see that we follow it consistently. Most of us plan to discipline a child, but carry it out inconsistently. Sometimes a spoon on the floor upsets us, so we spank. On other occasions, we are in a different mood and fail to discipline at all. On still another day, we may lose our temper or try to reason with a child. Since we change our tactics day by day, our children are confused, and our discipline is ineffective. By graphing misbehavior and carrying out our plan of discipline consistently, we can often see radical changes in short spans of time.

This book and *Help! I'm a Parent!* were written with classes and study groups in mind. The fourteen chapters can be covered in survey form in a one-quarter term of a Sunday school' class. By covering approximately one chapter in each book weekly, for example, the material can be studied in a twelve-week period. By taking one or two chapters monthly, a mother's study group or a gathering of married couples can cover a complete course in child rearing during the nine months of a school year. See chapter fourteen of *Help! I'm a Parent!* if further readings are desired. That chapter discusses three excellent books which can serve as collateral reading for parent study groups.

Now let's assume you have been asked to lead a study group. Your first response is something like this: "Wait a minute! I'm no expert. I have enough problems with my own children. I'd really like to learn myself, but I don't know enough to lead a group." If you feel that way, you may be just the person to guide a group through this material. This book isn't written to "be taught." It is intended to be experienced. The readings and assignments really stand by themselves. They do not need a set of lectures by a professional teacher. What is needed is a sensitive, sincere parent with a bent to study, an ability to relate to others, and a sincere desire to be a better parent.

Here are some suggestions for the first group meeting. After that, the basic pattern is established.

1. Begin by having every member introduce himself and tell a little about his children. It's good to ask each member why he came to the course and what he hopes to receive.

2. See that each person has a copy of this study guide as well as *Help! I'm a Parent!*

3. Outline the topics to be covered at each meeting and assign the specific chapters which discuss the topic. I suggest that you follow the sequence of the chapters in this book since they were designed for just this type of use.

4. To avoid having to lecture, take approximately fifteen minutes of the class period for reading chapter two of *Help! I'm a Parent!* It is not a long chapter and most will read it in ten or fifteen minutes. After everyone has finished, take a few minutes to review the basic ideas of that chapter. Then have everyone fill out Exercise I of chapter two of this book. That should take no more than ten minutes. In this way you have immediately

involved everyone in the class activities. A simple sharing of answers to Exercise I is a good close for the first session.

5. Arrange to phone each member once a week or have members phone each other. See that they have completed the next assignment and discuss any significant experiences either of you are having. This phoning may seem to be a nuisance at first, but we have found it is a key to the success of the course. It soon develops into a very stimulating discussion of successes and failures in applying the material.

After the first session, you are well on your way. The exercises carry the members step by step, and you need only to moderate the class discussions. Here are a few pointers for leading the discussion.

1. Encourage everyone to participate by calling on quiet ones to share their answers. I often ask each person in turn to relate his answer to one of the exercises.

2. Encourage members to share specific examples of their successes and failures. The successes encourage others and the failures give opportunity to clarify when techniques are being misapplied.

3. Be positive and complimentary when members are sharing.

4. After someone discusses an attempt at applying a new principle, ask others to evaluate their success. Encourage members to point out effective techniques and positive attitudes. Also see that they kindly but clearly mention weaknesses in the applications.

5. If one person tries to dominate the conversation, thank him for his comments and say something like, "Now, I'd like to know what Mary Lou has tried."

6. Maintain the attitude that the Bible is your ultimate authority. Encourage members to share relevant scriptural passages and principles.

7. Use the first few minutes of each meeting to review briefly the major points of the previous lesson.

8. Use the next portion of each meeting to discuss the attempted applications of the previous lesson's principles. Here is a good chance to have each person share one of his experiences.

9. If you decide not to present the new material in a lecture, simply make the next week's reading assignment and close the meeting. If you have meetings longer than one hour, it is often

good to take twenty or thirty minutes of each meeting for reading the next chapter and completing one of the next week's exercises. There are two reasons for this. Since most of us are busy and don't read much (especially men), you may get some to read more during that thirty minutes than the entire rest of the week. When you begin each new lesson by reading a chapter and completing one of the exercises, you also see that everyone gets started. The personal satisfaction of beginning a new lesson encourages everyone to carry out the rest of that week's work.

10. Establish the following principle: "Nobody can share or discuss his opinions unless he has completed *all* of that week's lesson." There are important reasons for this. First of all, some people like to talk about their own ideas. The purpose of this class is to discuss and apply basic biblical and psychological principles of this book, not to exchange pet peeves on various theories. By seeing that everyone who talks has read the material and completed the exercises, the tendency to stray is radically reduced. The restriction of communication to those who have finished the lessons also indicates to the members the importance you place on applying the material and it motivates them to do the work. Remember that we all tend to do as little as possible. Until your members do several of the exercises and see their value, they will want to come to listen rather than to do.

Chapter 2

THE GOALS OF MISBEHAVIOR[1]

No childish behavior is "purely accidental." Under every puzzling action is a motivating force. This chapter will help you learn the "why" of misbehavior. It reviews eight causes of behavior and applies this understanding to your children. The following table summarizes eight unseen causes of behavior.

TABLE 1

NEEDS AND GOALS

Genuine Emotional Needs	Substitute Goals	Reactions to Frustrated Needs and Goals
Confidence	Power and Control	Anger and Revenge
Love	Attention	Search for Psychological Safety
Worth	Perfection	

Feelings of love, confidence, and worth are healthy emotions. When children don't experience these positive feelings, they look for sub-

---

[1]This chapter is coordinated with "The Nature of Childhood," chapter two of *Help! I'm a Parent!*

stitute fulfillments. Being the center of attention helps hide a sense of loneliness. Controlling others by the use of power covers the anxiety caused by a lack of confidence. Becoming a "model child" defends against a feeling of unworthiness. In this sense, attention, power, and perfection are counterfeit reactions. They are our children's efforts to satisfy needs for love, confidence, and worth in a negative way. When the basic needs or their substitutes are not met, other dynamics come into play. The frustrated child turns to anger and revenge or to a variety of defense mechanisms to find psychological safety.

EXERCISE I

In the following examples, which of the eight causes of behavior seem to be operating? Notice that in each case the child has a legitimate need of confidence, love, or worth. But when these needs aren't met, he turns to misbehavior in a search for power, attention, perfection, revenge, or safety.[2]

1. An eleven-year-old "smart alec" who is continually disrupting his class.

    ----

2. A teenage girl who is excessively boy-crazy and is deeply hurt when rejected by the opposite sex.

    ----

3. An eight-year-old who is constantly bragging about how great he is.

    ----

4. A teenager who feels depressed and is constantly belittling herself.

---

[2]The answer key for Exercise I is at the end of this chapter.

5. A wife who is jealous of any women her husband meets.

----

6. A parent who spanks a child in anger for spilling milk at the dinner table.

----

7. A child who often says, "I'm bad" or, "I'm naughty."

----

8. A two-year-old who refuses to be toilet trained.

----

9. A husband who is discouraged with the quality of his work at the office.

----

10. A teenager who "accidentally" breaks a glass after being forced to wash the dishes.

----

11. A quiet ten-year-old who has few friends and seems afraid to enter in.

----

12. A seven-year-old who says, "Mommy, do you love me?"

----

13. A woman who feels she is a total failure as a wife and mother.

----

14. A child who throws a temper tantrum.

----

15. A husband who avoids involvement in the discipline of a child for fear of disagreements with his wife.

----

16. A competitive child who always has to win.

----

17. A perfectionistic woman whose house is always like a show-case.

----

18. A teenage girl who became pregnant to spite her parents.

----

19. A child who uses her lunch money to buy candy for her "friends."

----

20. A child who refuses to go to bed when asked.

EXERCISE II

Observe and briefly describe five instances of misbehavior for each of your children. What healthy emotional need (love, confidence, or worth) is he trying to meet? What substitute goal (attention, power, or perfection) does he mistakenly think will satisfy that need? Also, tell if he is looking for revenge or psychological safety through each behavior.

FIRST CHILD

1. Misbehavior --

   Need he is trying to meet --

   Substitute goal ---

   Is he also searching for revenge or safety? --------------------------------

   How? --

2. Misbehavior --

   Need he is trying to meet --

   Substitute goal ---

   Is he also searching for revenge or safety? --------------------------------

   How? --

3. Misbehavior --

   Need he is trying to meet --

   Substitute goal ---

   Is he also searching for revenge or safety? --------------------------------

   How? --

4. Misbehavior --

Need he is trying to meet --

Substitute goal --

Is he also searching for revenge or safety? --

How? --

5. Misbehavior --

Need he is trying to meet --

Substitute goal --

Is he also searching for revenge or safety? --

How? --

SECOND CHILD

1. Misbehavior --

Need he is trying to meet --

Substitute goal --

Is he also searching for revenge or safety? --

How? --

2. Misbehavior --

Need he is trying to meet --

Substitute goal --

Is he also searching for revenge or safety? ------------------------------

How? --

3. Misbehavior --

Need he is trying to meet --

Substitute goal --

Is he also searching for revenge or safety? ------------------------

How? --

4. Misbehavior --

Need he is trying to meet --

Substitute goal --

Is he also searching for revenge or safety? ------------------------

How? --

5. Misbehavior --

Need he is trying to meet --

Substitute goal --

Is he also searching for revenge or safety? ----------------------------------

How? --

THIRD CHILD

1. Misbehavior --

   Need he is trying to meet --

   Substitute goal ---

   Is he also searching for revenge or safety? ----------------------------------

   How? --

2. Misbehavior --

   Need he is trying to meet --

   Substitute goal ---

   Is he also searching for revenge or safety? ----------------------------------

   How? --

3. Misbehavior --

   Need he is trying to meet --

   Substitute goal ---

Is he also searching for revenge or safety? ----------------------------

How? ----------------------------

4. Misbehavior ----------------------------

Need he is trying to meet ----------------------------

Substitute goal ----------------------------

Is he also searching for revenge or safety? ----------------------------

How? ----------------------------

5. Misbehavior ----------------------------

Need he is trying to meet ----------------------------

Substitute goal ----------------------------

Is he also searching for revenge or safety? ----------------------------

How? ----------------------------

ANSWER KEY FOR EXERCISE I

1. Love and Attention
2. Love and Attention
3. Confidence and Power
4. Worth
5. Love and Attention
6. Revenge
7. Worth
8. Confidence and Power
9. Worth and Perfection
   (Possibly Confidence)
10. Revenge
11. Confidence and Psychological Safety
12. Love and Attention
13. Worth and Perfection
    (Possibly Confidence)
14. Revenge
15. Psychological Safety
16. Confidence and Power
17. Perfection and Worth
18. Revenge
19. Love and Attention
20. Confidence and Power

Chapter 3

CHILDHOOD HANGOVERS[1]

Chapter one of *Help! I'm a Parent!* introduced our approach to raising children by looking at some common family problems and the negative results of these conflicts. This chapter is designed to apply the insights of that chapter to your own family. Special emphasis is given to the influence of early childhood experiences on a child's relationship with God and on his adult personality adjustment. Here is a summary of the major ideas of chapter one of *Help! I'm a Parent!*

- Many parents and children are unable to enjoy each other because of frictions and frustrations.
- Children are learning maladaptive behavior patterns which will result in adjustment difficulties in later life.
- Some marriages are damaged because of disagreements involving children.
- Many of society's problems such as crime, rebellion, and mental illness spring from improper upbringing.
- Problems in parent-child relations may impair the child's ability to relate to God in a healthy way.

---

[1]This chapter is coordinated with "Parent to Parent" — chapter one of *Help! I'm a Parent!*

EXERCISE I (for wife)

Make a list of family conflicts which are frustrating to you or your children.

1. ---

2. ---

3. ---

4. ---

5. ---

EXERCISE I (for husband)

Make a list of family conflicts which are frustrating to you or your children.

1. ---

2. ---

3. ---

4. ---

5. ---

EXERCISE II (for wife)

A. Childhood experiences form our basic personality structure. Traits like hostility, depression, impulsiveness, worry, friendliness, optimism, warmth, criticalness, prejudiced attitudes, and social withdrawal all arise in childhood. To become more sensitive to these experiences, list five good personality traits which you learned in childhood.

1. *ability to sharing*

2. *how to be a friend*

3. _friendliness_

4. _____

5. _____

B. List five negative personality traits which you learned in childhood.

1. _prejudice_

2. _"judging"_

3. _____

4. _____

5. _____

EXERCISE II (for husband)

A. Childhood experiences form our basic personality structure. Traits like hostility, depression, impulsiveness, worry, friendliness, optimism, warmth, criticalness, prejudiced attitudes, and social withdrawal all arise in childhood. To become more sensitive to these experiences, list five good personality traits which you learned in childhood.

1. _friendship_

2. _Sharing_

3. _Companionships_

4. _courtesy_

5. _____

B. List five negative personality traits which you learned in childhood.

1. _prejudice_

2. _greed_

3. _Bad temper_

4. _Selfishness_

5. _worry_

EXERCISE III (for wife)

A. Children bring both joys and frustrations to family living. List five positive things you have gained personally from your experiences as a parent.

1. _____

2. _____

3. _____

4. _____

5. _____

B. List times when frustrations with your children have carried over into your relationship with your mate.

1. _____

2. _____

3. _____

4. _____

5. _____

EXERCISE III (for husband)

A. Children bring both joys and frustrations to family living. List five positive things you have gained personally from your experiences as a parent.

1. ---

2. ---

3. ---

4. ---

5. ---

B. List times when frustrations with your children have carried over into your relationship with your mate.

1. ---

2. ---

3. ---

4. ---

5. ---

EXERCISE IV (for wife)

This exercise is a sentence-completion test. It will help you understand yourself and the relationship between your attitudes toward life, your parents, and God. Please finish each sentence with the first thought that comes to mind.

1. I pleased my friends when *I'm me*

2. I am happy *when Ken + I are close*

3. My father should have *been more loving (patient)*

4. Love is *kind*

5. When I was a child ⸻

6. Sometimes I feel the Lord _loves me_

7. I became angry when _my kids disobey me_

8. My father and I _were close_

9. A good parent _loves his kids_

10. Bible reading seems _important_

11. I wish God ⸻

12. My mother _means a lot to me_

13. My husband _I love very much_

14. More than anything I need _understanding_ _patience_

15. Sometimes when I pray _I don't want to_

16. Talking with people _is enjoyable_

17. I often wish for _better rapport with others_

18. I feel that my parents _loved me_

19. When I think of Jesus Christ _I think of a best friend who truly loves me_

20. People in authority _should be respected_

21. The best thing about my parents _was their love & concern_

22. I feel guilty _when I'm selfish_

23. I feel that God _loves me_

24. I was depressed _yesterday_

25. I felt closest to my father when _we were together_

26. Sometimes my mother *bothers me*

27. At times I *feel guilty*

28. I get angry at God *at times*

29. When my father disciplined me *I listened*

30. Most mothers *are patient*

31. Prayer *is important to me*

32. When my father and I talked *I loved him more* *I felt a special closeness)*

33. A husband should *love his family*

34. My spiritual life *is not what it should be*

35. Taking orders *is necessary.*

36. I became angry when my parents *didn't understand me.*

37. Father

38. When I am depressed, God seems *concerned.*

39. I dislike people who *are snotty*

40. My mother should have *been a Christian*

41. The Lord *loves me*

42. I am upset by

43. When I think of mother *I think of love*

44. When God disciplines *He loves me*

45. I wanted my mother to *be a J.*

46. I like to daydream *too much.*

47. I feel closest to God when _I'm happy_

48. If I could have changed my parents _they'd have been ??_

49. My mother and father _mean a lot to me_

50. The thing I like most about God _His forgivefulness_

EXERCISE IV (for husband)

This exercise is a sentence-completion test. It will help you understand yourself and the relationship between your attitudes toward life, your parents, and God. Please finish each sentence with the first thought that comes to mind.

1. I pleased my friends when _I'm natural_

2. I am happy _when I'm relaxed_

3. My father should have _____

4. Love is _understanding_

5. When I was a child _I had fun_

6. Sometimes I feel the Lord _ignores me_

7. I became angry when _I'm rushed_

8. My father and I _have a good relationship_

9. A good parent _is loving_

10. Bible reading seems _difficult at times_

11. I wish God _____

12. My mother _is understanding_

13. My wife _is loving and considerate_

31

14. More than anything I need *is confidence*

15. Sometimes when I pray

16. Talking with people *is hard*

17. I often wish for *patience*

18. I feel that my parents *are kind to me*

19. When I think of Jesus Christ

20. People in authority *need discipline*

21. The best thing about my parents *is their love*

22. I feel guilty *when I lose my temper*

23. I feel that God *loves me.*

24. I was depressed *most of my life*

25. I felt closest to my father when *I talked with him*

26. Sometimes my mother *is too understanding*

27. At times I *am too nervous*

28. I get angry at God

29. When my father disciplined me *I listened*

30. Most mothers *care*

31. Prayer *helps*

32. When my father and I talked *it helped me*

33. A wife should *love her husband*

34. My spiritual life *needs discipline*

35. Taking orders ___needs___ _____

36. I became angry when my parents _____

37. Father _____

38. When I am depressed, God seems _____

39. I dislike people who _____

40. My mother should have _____

41. The Lord _____

42. I am upset by _____

43. When I think of mother _____

44. When God disciplines _____

45. I wanted my mother to _____

46. I like to daydream _____

47. I feel closest to God when _____

48. If I could have changed my parents _____

49. My mother and father _____

50. The thing I like most about God _____

The sentence-completion test you just completed is called a projective test. This means that we "project" our own personal feelings and thoughts into our answers. Read over your answers and see what they tell about your personality. Give special attention to the responses you gave to the sentences referring to God and to your parents. We usually find interesting similarities between these answers. People who feel depressed and guilty because of their relations with their parents often picture God as distant or feel they are a failure in their

Christian life. On a similar test one woman finished some of her sentences this way:

My Father	*was a stranger*
My church	*is large*
Bible reading	*is often depressing*
I pray	*sometimes*
My parents	*gave me up*
My spiritual life	*is at a standstill*
Christian friends	*are shallow*
My mother	*was unhappy*

This woman's bad experiences with her parents caused her spiritual life to seem shallow and depressing. Just as she viewed her parents as cold and rejecting, she saw the church as large (probably indicating she felt lonely there), Christians as shallow, and prayer as not very meaningful.

Most of our responses are not as vivid as these. But we can gain insight by studying our answers. This exercise will help you understand yourself and make you sensitive to your children's feelings. Here are a few guidelines for evaluating your sentences.

– Any sentence that is left blank implies "psychological blocking." This means you do not feel free to respond spontaneously to the topic of the sentence. This also applies to those who have lost a parent. "Blocking" on a sentence item such as "When I think of mother" may mean you are unconsciously inhibiting negative or upsetting feelings in relation to your mother.
– Strong words such as "fear," "anger," or "discouragement" may indicate important negative emotions.
– The use of similar words or phrases in describing God and your own parents is important.
– Which parent do your sentences indicate you have the most positive feelings for?
– Superficial answers indicate a defensiveness about facing your own negative feelings. Some people answer nearly every item in an ideal way, such as: "I am happy *all the time*", "When I was a child *I was happy*", "Sometimes I feel the Lord *is great*", "My

father and I *were close*", "My mother *was a good mother*", "I feel that my parents *were happily married*". Nobody's life is perfectly happy and no parents are perfect. An emotionally mature person is able to have a positive approach to life, his family, his parents, and God. But he is also free to see areas of conflict and personal frustration. If your answers are "too good," you may want to ask yourself why you need to deny any possible problem areas.
– Areas that depress or frustrate you are especially important.

EXERCISE V (for wife)

A. Here is another way of seeing the influence of childhood experiences on your image of God. Circle the statement which most nearly describes your feelings. But be careful. Those of us without serious emotional problems often experience a "halo effect." On exercises like this we tend to mark most items above average. We choose our answers on the basis of what we think should be, or on the basis of our intellectual reasoning. For this exercise to be helpful, you must answer with your *feelings*, not with your *thoughts*. For example, we all "know" God loves us. But most of us have times when we don't "feel" His love. Select your answers according to your feelings.

1. Relationship to Mother

Communication:
1. Rarely had good communication
2. Communicated, but often on a superficial level
3. Communicated frequently and meaningfully

Emotional Warmth:
1. Cold and distant
2. Slightly cold and distant
3. Cordial, but not warm
4. Moderately warm and close
5. Very warm and close

Discipline:
1. Lax and insufficient
2. Firm, but sometimes harsh or inconsistent
3. Firm but loving
4. Overly strict

	5. Moderate controls based on mutual respect
Acceptance:	1. Felt continually rejected
	2. Felt accepted only when performance was good
	3. Usually felt accepted
	4. Continually felt accepted
Mother's Satisfaction With Performance:	1. Rarely pleased with me
	2. Occasionally pleased with me
	3. Often pleased with me
	4. Nearly always pleased with me
Mother's Emotional Control:	1. Often lost her temper
	2. Occasionally lost her temper
	3. Rarely lost her temper
Mother's Emotional Outlook:	1. Always optimistic and happy
	2. Usually optimistic and happy
	3. Often moody and depressed
	4. Usually depressed and moody

2. Relationship to Father

Communication:	1. Rarely had good communication
	2. Communicated, but often on a superficial level
	3. Communicated frequently and meaningfully
Emotional Warmth:	1. Cold and distant
	2. Slightly cold and distant
	3. Cordial, but not very warm
	4. Moderately warm and close
	5. Very warm and close
Discipline:	1. Lax and insufficient
	2. Firm, but sometimes harsh or inconsistent
	3. Firm but loving
	4. Overly strict
	5. Moderate controls based on mutual respect

Acceptance:	1. Felt continually rejected 2. Felt accepted only when performance was good (3.) Usually felt accepted 4. Continually felt accepted
Father's Satisfaction With Peformance:	1. Rarely pleased with me (2.) Occasionally pleased with me 3. Often pleased with me 4. Nearly always pleased with me
Father's Emotional Control:	(1.) Often lost his temper 2. Occasionally lost his temper 3. Rarely lost his temper
Father's Emotional Outlook:	1. Always optimistic and happy 2. Usually optimistic and happy (3.) Often moody and depressed 4. Usually depressed and moody

3. Relationship with God

Communication:	1. Rarely have good communication through prayer or Bible study (2.) Communicate, but often on a superficial level (3.) Communicate frequently and meaningfully
Emotional Relationship With God:	1. Seems very cold and distant 2. Slightly cold and distant 3. Cordial, but not warm 4. Moderately warm and close (5.) Very warm and close
Feeling Toward God's Discipline:	1. Seems insufficient 2. Seems firm, but sometimes harsh and inconsistent 3. Seems firm but loving 4. Seems harsh at times 5. Seems adequate and appears to be based on respect
Feelings About God's Acceptance:	1. Feel accepted only when I perform 2. Feel continually rejected

3. Usually feel accepted
4. Always feel accepted

God's
Emotional Attitude:

1. Feel God is often angry with me
2. Feel God is occasionally upset with me
3. Feel God is disappointed with me
4. Feel God is satisfied with me

B. You have now finished two exercises designed to help you gain insight into your own feelings and your emotional reactions to God. Keeping these exercises in mind, list five of the most positive aspects of your feelings toward God.

1. _He loves me_

2. _He is forgiving_

3. _I can go to Him_

4. _He wants me to come to Him_

5. _____

C. List five circumstances where you have difficulty experiencing a vital relationship with Christ.

1. _When I wrong, but don't want to_

2. _change. I'm feeling lukewarm_

3. _____

4. _____

5. _____

D. Now that you have finished the sentence completions and the rating scale on your relations with your parents, study your answers to get new self-understanding. As you do this, you will be in a better position to meet your child's emotional and spiritual needs. Do you notice similarities between any of your attitudes to God and to your earthly parents? ---------------------- What are they?

1. _superfic_____commun_____
2. _ful accepted when doing right_
3. _____
4. _____
5. _____

E. What do you think has caused you to develop these similar feelings?

_My relationsh_____with my_
parents has affected my rel.
with God more than I ever
realized

EXERCISE V (for husband)

A. Here is another way of seeing the influence of childhood experiences on your image of God. Circle the statement which most nearly describes your relationship with your parents. But be careful. Those of us without serious emotional problems often experience a "halo effect." On exercises like this we tend to mark most items above average. We choose our answers on the basis of what we think should be, or on the basis of our intellectual reasoning. For this exercise to be helpful, you must answer with your *feelings*, not with your *thoughts*. For example, we all "know" God loves us. But most of us have times when we don't "feel" His love. Select your answers according to your feelings.

1. Relationship to Mother
   Communication: 1. Rarely had good communication

Emotional Warmth:
2. Communicated, but often on a superficial level
3. Communicated frequently and meaningfully

Emotional Warmth:
1. Cold and distant
2. Slightly cold and distant
3. Cordial, but not warm
4. Moderately warm and close
5. Very warm and close

Discipline:
1. Lax and insufficient
2. Firm, but sometimes harsh or inconsistent
3. Firm but loving
4. Overly strict
5. Moderate controls based on mutual respect

Acceptance:
1. Felt continually rejected
2. Felt accepted only when performance was good
3. Usually felt accepted
4. Continually felt accepted

Mother's Satisfaction With Performance:
1. Rarely pleased with me
2. Occasionally pleased with me
3. Often pleased with me
4. Nearly always pleased with me

Mother's Emotional Control:
1. Often lost her temper
2. Occasionally lost her temper
3. Rarely lost her temper

Mother's Emotional Outlook:
1. Always optimistic and happy
2. Usually optimistic and happy
3. Often moody and depressed
4. Usually depressed and moody

2. Relationship to Father

Communication:
1. Rarely had good communication
2. Communicated, but often on a superficial level

	3. Communicated frequently and meaningfully
Emotional Warmth:	1. Cold and distant
	2. Slightly cold and distant
	3. Cordial, but not very warm
	4. Moderately warm and close
	5. Very warm and close

Discipline:

1. Lax and insufficient
2. Firm, but sometimes harsh or inconsistent
3. Firm but loving
4. Overly strict
5. Moderate controls based on mutual respect

Acceptance:

1. Felt continually rejected
2. Felt accepted only when performance was good
3. Usually felt accepted
4. Continually felt accepted

Father's Satisfaction With Performance:

1. Rarely pleased with me
2. Occasionally pleased with me
3. Often pleased with me
4. Nearly always pleased with me

Father's Emotional Control:

1. Often lost his temper
2. Occasionally lost his temper
3. Rarely lost his temper

Father's Emotional Outlook:

1. Always optimistic and happy
2. Usually optimistic and happy
3. Often moody and depressed
4. Usually depressed and moody

3. Relationship with God

Communication:

1. Rarely have good communication through prayer or Bible study
2. Communicate, but often on a superficial level
3. Communicate frequently and meaningfully

Emotional Relationship With God:	1. Seems very cold and distant
	2. Slightly cold and distant
	3. Cordial, but not warm
	4. Moderately warm and close
	5. Very warm and close
Feeling Toward God's Discipline:	1. Seems insufficient
	2. Seems firm, but sometimes harsh and inconsistent
	3. Seems firm but loving
	4. Seems harsh at times
	5. Seems adequate and appears to be based on respect
Feelings About God's Acceptance:	1. Feel accepted only when I perform
	2. Feel continually rejected
	3. Usually feel accepted
	4. Always feel accepted
God's Emotional Attitude:	1. Feel God is often angry with me
	2. Feel God is occasionally upset with me
	3. Feel God is disappointed with me
	4. Feel God is satisfied with me

B. You have now finished two exercises designed to help you gain insight into your own feelings and your emotional reactions to God. Keeping these exercises in mind, list five of the most positive aspects of your feelings toward God.

1. --

2. --

3. --

4. --

5. --

C. List five circumstances where you have difficulty experiencing a vital relationship with Christ.

42

1. --

2. --

3. --

4. --

5. --

D. Now that you have finished the sentence completions and the rating scale on your relations with your parents, study your answers to get new self-understanding. As you do this, you will be in a better position to meet your child's emotional spiritual needs. Do you notice similarities between any of your attitudes to God and to your earthly parents? ---------------------- What are they?

1. --

2. --

3. --

4. --

5. --

E. What do you think has caused you to develop these similar feelings?

EXERCISE VI

A. Every child's image of God is strongly influenced by his relationship with his parents. What are some positive attributes of God your child is learning from his relationship with you?

1. --

2. --

3. --

4. --

5. --

B. What are some negative attitudes toward God your child may be developing?

1. --

2. --

3. --

4. --

5. --

C. Which of your reactions do you need to change to help your child develop a more positive image of God?

1. --

2. --

3. --

4. --

5. --

Chapter 4

GOD, THE MODEL PARENT[1]

The family is not a temporary sociological phenomenon. It is essential to God's plan for the human race. God designed the family for four major reasons:

- To meet the physical, spiritual and emotional needs of every family member.
- To teach each family member about God's attributes of love, justice and righteousness through the human example of other family members.
- To guide and to train children since they have rebellious natures and need parental guidance.
- To teach respect for authority which is the foundation of our society.

As our "Heavenly Father," God has set us an example of the perfect parent. We can learn effective ways of rearing our children by patterning our parental roles from His example.

- In training His children, God uses discipline but does not punish. Following His example, we should discipline our children but never punish them. The following table summarizes the differences between discipline and punishment.

---

[1]This chapter is coordinated with "Discipline's Divine Design," chapter three of *Help! I'm a Parent!*

TABLE 2

	Punishment	Discipline
Purpose	To inflict penalty for an offense	To train for correction and maturity
Focus	Past misdeeds	Future correct deeds
Attitude	Hostility and frustration on the part of the parent	Love and concern on the part of the parent
Resulting Emotion in the Child	Fear and guilt	Security

– God never motivates His sons by fear. He earns our respect by the loving exercise of His authority. He doesn't try to "win" respect by overwhelming us with power. Like God, we should never motivate our children out of fear. We should earn their respect, not fight to "win" it.

– God never ventilates His anger on His children. Likewise, we should never vent our frustrations on our children.

EXERCISE I

Here are two biblical passages demonstrating God's methods and attitudes in dicipline. After reading each incident, list the insights you gained from God's attitude, His methods of motivation and His goals in disciplining. Several of these insights are listed in the answer key at the end of the chapter.

1. John 8:3-11

And the scribes and Pharisees brought unto him a woman taken in adultery; and when they had set her in the midst, they say unto him, Master, this woman was taken in adultery, in the very act. Now Moses in the law commanded us, that such should be stoned: but what sayest thou? This they said, tempting him, that they might have to accuse him. But Jesus stooped down, and with *his* finger wrote on the ground, *as though he heard them not.* So when they continued asking him, he lifted up himself, and said unto them, He that is without sin among you, let him first cast a stone at her. And again he stooped down, and wrote on the ground. And they which heard *it,* being convicted by *their own* conscience, went out one by one, beginning at the eldest, *even* unto the last: and Jesus was left alone, and the woman standing in the midst. When Jesus had lifted up himself, and saw none but the woman, he said unto her, Woman, where are those thine accusers? hath no man condemned thee? She said, No man, Lord. And Jesus said unto her, Neither do I condemn thee: go, and sin no more.

What specific examples does Christ set which can apply to your children?

1. --

2. --

3. --

4. --

5. --

2. Luke 15:11-24

And he said, A certain man had two sons: and the younger of them said to *his* father, Father, give me the portion of goods that falleth *to me*. And he divided unto them *his* living. And not many days after the younger son gathered all together, and took his journey into a far country, and there wasted his substance with riotous living. And when he had spent all, there arose a mighty famine in that land; and he began to be in want. And he went and joined himself to a citizen of that country; and he sent him into his fields to feed swine. And he would fain have filled his belly with the husks that the swine did eat: and no man gave unto him. And when he came to himself, he said, How many hired servants of my father's have bread enough and to spare, and I perish with hunger! I will arise and go to my father, and will say unto him, Father, I have sinned against heaven, and before thee, and am no more worthy to be called thy son: make me as one of thy hired servants. And he arose, and came to his father. But when he was yet a great way off, his father saw him, and had compassion, and ran, and fell on his neck, and kissed him. And the son said unto him, Father, I have sinned against heaven, and in thy sight, and am no more worthy to be called thy son. But the father said to his servants, Bring forth the best robe, and put *it* on him; and put a ring on his hand, and shoes on *his* feet: and bring hither the fatted calf, and kill *it;* and let us eat, and be merry: for this my son was dead, and is alive again; he was lost, and is found. And they began to be merry.

What specific examples does this father set which can apply to your children?

1. _____

2. _____

3. _____

4. _____

5. _____

EXERCISE II (for wife)

One of the biggest mistakes we make as parents is to get upset and punish children instead of training them in love. List three times when you punished your children in anger rather than disciplined in love. Tell why the misbehavior made you angry, your negative reaction, and how you could have disciplined effectively.

1. Child's behavior which made you angry _____

_____

   a. Your negative reaction _____

_____

   b. Why did the misbehavior make you angry? _____

_____

_____

   c. How could you have disciplined your child effectively? _____

_____

_____

2. Child's behavior which made you angry _____

_____

a. Your negative reaction --

----

b. Why did the misbehavior make you angry? ----------------------

----

----

c. How could you have disciplined your child effectively? --------

----

----

3. Child's behavior which made you angry ----------------------------

----

a. Your negative reaction --

----

b. Why did the misbehavior make you angry? ----------------------

----

----

c. How could you have disciplined your child effectively? --------

----

EXERCISE II (for husband)

In completing the following exercise, recall three times when you punished your children in anger rather than disciplined in love.

1. Child's behavior which made you angry --

----

   a. Your negative reaction ---

      ----

   b. Why did the misbehavior make you angry? -----------------------

      ----

      ----

   c. How could you have disciplined your child effectively? --------

      ----

      ----

2. Child's behavior which made you angry --

----

   a. Your negative reaction ---

      ----

   b. Why did the misbehavior make you angry? -----------------------

      ----

      ----

   c. How could you have disciplined your child effectively? --------

      ----

      ----

3. Child's behavior which made you angry --------------------------------------

----

a. Your negative reaction ---

----

b. Why did the misbehavior make you angry? -------------------------

----

----

c. How could you have disciplined your child effectively? --------

----

EXERCISE III (for wife)

Most of us have some "emotional hangovers" from childhood. Since our parents used fear and guilt to scare us into good behavior, we are in the habit of using this method on our children. But this is wrong. Fear is an unhealthy motivation. To understand this point, think of the most frightening thing your parents ever did to you. Can you remember your reactions? I imagine you shaped up immediately! But what about your feelings? Can you recall your inner emotions? Didn't that fear continue to haunt you on occasion in the future? On the next few lines describe that experience and the feelings you remember. It may also be good to discuss this with your mate.

51

EXERCISE III (for husband)

Discuss your most frightening experience with your parents.

EXERCISE IV

When we want our children to "shape up" immediately, we are often tempted to yell, spank, or in some other way scare them into good behavior. This motivation by fear is contrary to biblical teaching. Although it may give the temporary behavior we desire, it tears at our children's confidence and leads to continuous anxiety. Getting proper behavior is not our only goal. When we use fear to obtain proper actions, we are actually causing serious inner emotional problems to develop. These feelings may not be obvious at first. But as you study your child's reactions to your discipline, look for indications of fearfulness and tension. You can soon begin to detect the negative results of fear motivation. To develop better ways of discipline, make a list of five times you tried to motivate your child by fear. In each case list your child's original misbehavior, the way in which you attempted to motivate by fear, your child's behavioral response, your child's apparent inner emotional response, and a better way you could have motivated him.

1. Child's misbehavior --

   ----

   a. How did you motivate out of fear? --------------------------------

      ----

      ----

   b. What was your tone of voice? -------------------------------------

   c. What was your child's behavioral response? --------------------

      ----

      ----

   d. What was your child's inner emotional response? --------------

      ----

      ----

   e. How could you have motivated a better way? -------------------

      ----

      ----

2. Child's misbehavior --

   ----

   a. How did you motivate out of fear? --------------------------------

      ----

      ----

b. What was your tone of voice? -------------------------------------

c. What was your child's behavioral response? -----------------------

----

----

d. What was your child's inner emotional response? --------------

----

----

e. How could you have motivated a better way? ---------------------

----

----

3. Child's misbehavior --

----

a. How did you motivate out of fear? -------------------------------

----

----

b. What was your tone of voice? -------------------------------------

c. What was your child's behavioral response? -----------------------

----

----

d. What was your child's inner emotional response? --------------

----

----

e. How could you have motivated a better way? -----------------

----

----

4. Child's misbehavior ----------------

----

a. How did you motivate out of fear? ----------------

----

b. What was your tone of voice? ----------------

c. What was your child's behavioral response? ----------------

----

----

d. What was your child's inner emotional response? ----------------

----

----

e. How could you have motivated a better way? ----------------

----

----

5. Child's misbehavior ----------------

----

a. How did you motivate out of fear? ....

....

....

b. What was your tone of voice? ....

c. What was your child's behavioral response? ....

....

....

d. What was your child's inner emotional response? ....

....

....

e. How could you have motivated a better way? ....

....

....

ANSWER KEY FOR EXERCISE I

Woman Taken in Adultery

1. Christ didn't get angry at the woman.
2. Christ didn't condemn her or motivate by guilt or fear.
3. Christ's attitude was loving and accepting.
4. Christ didn't focus on the past sinful behavior but on her future good behavior.

Prodigal Son

1. He didn't motivate the son by fear when the son decided to leave.
2. He didn't force the son to stay. He let him grow up and assume responsibility for his behavior.
3. He accepted the son with a loving attitude and with no condemnation even though the son had been sinning.
4. He didn't focus on the son's past.

Chapter 5

HOW MISBEHAVIOR IS LEARNED[1]

The main theme of this chapter is that children develop and maintain behaviors that are rewarding. Actions which are not rewarded tend to be extinguished. The specific principles involved in this process are:

- Actions that are rewarded or reinforced are more likely to be repeated in the future.
- Behaviors that are not rewarded tend to weaken and become extinguished.
- A reinforcement may be anything that satisfies a child's goal or leads to pleasure.
- A social reinforcer is any aspect of a human relationship which has a positive value to the child.
- A nonsocial reinforcer is any nonhuman object or experience which the child enjoys.
- Actions that stop painful or negative experiences also serve as reinforcers.
- To be most effective, reinforcements should come soon after the desired behavior.
- When your child is learning a new behavior, it is important to reward him every time he performs the desired behavior.

---

[1]This chapter is coordinated with "Problems Don't Just Happen," chapter four of *Help! I'm a Parent!*

– After desirable behavior is well established, it should be reinforced only occasionally.
– When a child is learning new behaviors, it often helps if we break a large task into smaller steps and give reinforcement after each one.
– We often unconsciously reinforce our children's undesirable behaviors even though we don't approve of such behavior.
– Our children may reinforce our undesirable behavior and promote continued family problems.
– Children also learn by imitating the behavior of parents and others.

EXERCISE I

In the following examples, see how you could be rewarding your child for good or bad behavior.[2]

1. You have just told your son he is not allowed to have candy before supper. He cries hysterically and you can't stand the noise. Finally you say, "O.K., but just this once."

   a. How did you reinforce your son's crying?

   ----

   b. What is likely to happen next time you tell him he may not have candy? --

2. Your ten-year-old spontaneously helped clear the supper dishes. You say, "Thanks for clearing the table, Mary. Since I'm through with dishes early, let's go work on the new dress we're making for you."

   a. How did you reward your daughter's positive behavior?

---

[2]See key at the end of this chapter for correct answers.

----

b. What is more likely to happen tomorrow night after supper?

----

3. You are sitting quietly on the couch when your ten-year-old yells, "Mother, he hit me!" "Stop it, Peter," you exclaim; "you know better than that!"

a. What motivation prompted Peter to hit his sister?

----

b. Did you reinforce that behavior? ---------------------- If so, how?

----

c. What is likely to happen next time Peter wants attention?

----

4. As you walk downtown, your son continually lags behind. You tell him to hurry, but you stop and wait until he finally catches up.

a. How are you reinforcing his lagging?

----

b. What could you do that would not reward his lagging and would extinguish this undesirable behavior?

----

5. In getting ready for Sunday school each week, you get frustrated and upset. You yell at the kids, "Hurry up or we'll be late again!" Every week you go through this same hassle. Soon your children start showing the same frustrations you have.

   How did your child learn that behavior?

EXERCISE II

A. Marsha was a "crying child." When she didn't get her way, she cried. When the baby-sitter came, she cried. When she was put to bed, she cried. This exercise will help you understand the "crying child." It will also help you learn to change other types of misbehavior.[3]

1. Children are motivated to cry by the same eight goals which cause all behavior. For review, list those eight motivating goals.

   a. --

   b. --

   c. --

   d. --

   e. --

   f. --

---

[3]See key at the end of this chapter for correct answers.

g. ---

h. ---

2. When Marsha didn't get her way, she cried. What goals were motivating her?

   a. --

   b. --

3. When Marsha's parents left her with a sitter, she always cried. What two goals were probably motivating her to cry?

   a. --

   b. --

4. When Marsha was put to bed, she said she was afraid and cried. Which three goals were most likely causing her to cry?

   a. --

   b. --

   c. --

B. We often unknowingly reward our children's misbehavior. Since actions don't continue without reinforcement, Marsha's parents must be doing things which satisfy her attempts to gain power, attention, revenge, or psychological safety through crying.

1. List two or three things Marsha's parents might be doing that reward her for crying when she doesn't get her way.

   a. --

   b. --

   c. --

2. List three or four things Marsha's parents might be doing that reinforce her crying when she is left with a baby-sitter.

    a. --

    b. --

    c. --

    d. --

3. List two or three things Marsha's parents might be doing that reward her crying when she's put to bed.

    a. --

    b. --

    c. --

C. The first step in overcoming negative behavior is plotting the bad behaviors. Marsha's parents could make a chart like this:

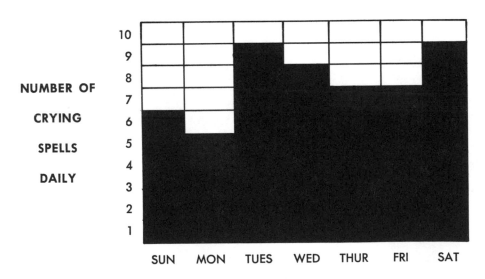

This chart shows that Marsha usually cried between five and nine times daily. If you have problems with your child's crying, fill out the empty chart to study his behavior.

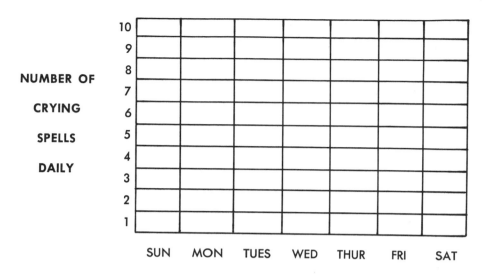

NUMBER OF CRYING SPELLS DAILY

10 9 8 7 6 5 4 3 2 1

SUN   MON   TUES   WED   THUR   FRI   SAT

D. The second step in breaking bad habits is to meet your child's needs for love, confidence, and worth in a healthy way. This makes it unnecessary for him to turn to misbehavior.

  1. How could Marsha's parents meet her needs for a sense of confidence and love so she wouldn't turn to crying every time something went wrong?

   a. --

   b. --

   c. --

   d. --

   e. --

   f. --

   g. --

   h. --

   i. --

E. The third step in changing misbehavior is to eliminate the rewards your child is gaining. This starts to extinguish negative behavior.

1. To eliminate the rewards Marsha gets for crying when she doesn't get her way, what should Marsha's parents stop doing?

   a. ---

   b. ---

   c. ---

2. To eliminate the rewards Marsha gets for crying when left with a sitter, what should Marsha's parents and the sitter stop doing?

   a. ---

   b. ---

   c. ---

   d. ---

3. To eliminate the rewards Marsha gets for crying when put to bed, what should her parents stop doing?

   a. ---

   b. ---

   c. ---

F. The last step in breaking the crying habit is to reward more desirable reactions. The first time Marsha doesn't cry when her parents don't let her have her way, they should reinforce this good behavior. One way of rewarding Marsha would be to listen carefully to what she is saying after she is told she cannot have her way. Since she may be expressing a genuine wish, Marsha's parents might say, "We're glad we can talk about this nicely," and give her a hug. The compliment and hug would be social reinforcers. If Marsha had been told she was not allowed to go outside and play, and for a change didn't break into tears, one of her parents could say, "But I would like to play inside with you awhile. What could we do together?" This unexpected play time would be a good reward for not crying.

1. Now that we have seen the importance of rewarding noncrying behavior, let's apply this principle to Marsha's other problem times. If Marsha forgot to cry when her parents left, she should be reinforced immediately. List some social and nonsocial reinforcers Marsha's parents and baby-sitter could give to reward her good behavior.

    a. --

    b. --

    c. --

    d. --

    e. --

2. If Marsha went to bed quietly one night, how could this behavior be rewarded?

    a. --

    b. --

    c. --

    d. --

G. When Marsha's parents put their new methods of discipline into practice, they should keep a record of their progress. If you are working on a crying problem, use this empty chart to look for your "Marsha's" progress.

	SUN	MON	TUES	WED	THUR	FRI	SAT
10							
9							
8							
7							
6							
5							
4							
3							
2							
1							

NUMBER OF CRYING SPELLS DAILY

EXERCISE III

A. In Exercise II, chapter two, you described five instances of your child's misbehavior. Analyze those situations and write out the rewards you have unknowingly been giving your child.

1. Rewards the first child is receiving for bad behavior.

   a. --

   ----

   b. --

   ----

   c. --

   ----

   d. --

   ----

   e. --

   ----

2. Rewards the second child is receiving for bad behavior.

   a. _____

   _____

   b. _____

   _____

   c. _____

   _____

   d. _____

   _____

   e. _____

   _____

3. Rewards the third child is receiving for bad behavior.

   a. _____

   _____

   b. _____

   _____

   c. _____

   _____

   d. _____

   _____

   e. _____

   _____

B. Some rewards work well for some children, but not for others. To develop a plan for changing your child's behavior, it is essential to know what rewards are most effective for each child. List the five rewards that seem most effective in shaping each child's behavior. You can determine these rewards by observing his behavior. What does he spontaneously do and ask for? These are probably the things he finds rewarding. These rewards may be either social or nonsocial reinforcers.

1. Oldest child

    a. --

    b. --

    c. --

    d. --

    e. --

2. Middle child

    a. --

    b. --

    c. --

    d. --

    e. --

3. Youngest child

    a. --

    b. --

    c. --

    d. --

    e. --

EXERCISE IV

Changing a specific behavior

Maybe your child's problem isn't crying. In this exercise you are to pick one of your children's problem behaviors which you would like to change through the principles of reinforcement and extinction. Whining, temper tantrums, and mealtime misconduct are three behaviors which usually respond well to this method of training. Your first step is to pick one specific behavior you want to change. Don't start with more than one. When parents try to change several things at once, it usually doesn't work. By focusing on one problem behavior, you can plan your method of discipline carefully and your child can understand the process. It is also important to be specific. Some parents say, "We want to improve his table manners." That will rarely work because it is too vague. Improved table manners might mean sitting still, saying "please," talking quietly, not fighting with sister, or eating all of the food. We should pick one of these specific behaviors. For a beginning, we might say, "I want to teach Johnny to say 'please' every time he asks for something." After Johnny learns this habit, you may say, "I want Johnny to stop kicking his sister under the table." In this way we work out one problem at a time.

Now a couple of words of warning. When you first apply any new principle, a child's reaction is often to test you out. If you decide to extinguish temper tantrums by ignoring this behavior, you should expect the next tantrum or two to be even worse. Your child is afraid of losing a powerful weapon and he won't quit easily! You should brace yourself for a few more kicks and some louder screams! Only when he finds out you intend to stick to your new methods will the tantrums cease.

Consistency is another key word. Once you decide to ignore them, you must ignore them all. If you give in just once, you ruin your chances. Instead of teaching your child, "Tantrums never work," you teach him to realize, "Even though mom and dad are trying a new approach, they will give in if I yell loud enough and long enough. Therefore, I must yell louder and longer." You have actually increased the likelihood of tantrums by being inconsistent!

With this preparation, we are ready to begin. Select one specific problem you want to change. Follow each of the steps outlined below and watch the results!

1. Describe the specific behavior you want to change ----------------

    ----

    ----

2. For a period of one week (before you start the new discipline) record the frequency of this behavior. This pre-recording is essential. The temptation is to try to change things without studying them carefully beforehand. Avoid that temptation and carefully record every occurrence of the behavior you have chosen to change.

	10							
	9							
	8							
NUMBER OF	7							
MISBEHAVIORS	6							
DAILY	5							
	4							
	3							
	2							
	1							
		SUN	MON	TUES	WED	THUR	FRI	SAT

3. The next step in breaking a bad habit is to see if there is an unmet need for love, confidence, or worth which you can meet in a healthy way. Which of the eight motivators seem to be causing the misbehavior? --

    How can you meet these needs so your child won't have to turn to misbehavior? ---

    ----

----

4. The fourth step in changing misbehavior is to eliminate the rewards your child is getting for the bad behavior. List the rewards you have unconsciously been giving your child for misbehavior. --

----

----

5. The last step in changing undesirable behavior is to reinforce a good behavior which competes with the undesirable reaction. When a child says, "Please pass the butter," in a pleasant voice, he can't be asking impolitely at the same time. By rewarding politeness, we may help eliminate impoliteness, because they can't exist together.

6. The day you begin the new procedures of extinction and reward, start a new chart of misbehavior. Record each occurrence of the bad behavior so you can compare it with the first chart and look for improvement.

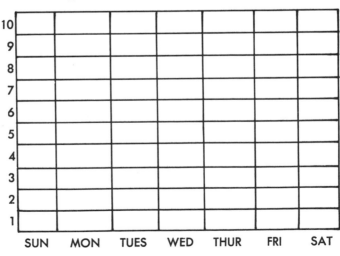

Most behaviors begin to change after the first few days of a new type of discipline. A few long-entrenched habits may take weeks to alter. Remember to be consistent and stick to it. If you don't see progress after two weeks, re-evaluate your method by asking these three questions:

Is my child getting some reinforcement (such as attention or revenge) which I didn't recognize? --

----

Are the rewards I am using to encourage good behavior really things my child finds rewarding? --

----

What is my attitude while disciplining? --

In nearly every instance of failure, the child is getting either some unknown reward for bad behavior or an insufficient reward for good behavior. When we are disciplining out of anger or frustration, all forms of discipline may fail. The child knows he is winning a power struggle by upsetting us and he finds this reinforcing. If rewards and extinction still don't work, try some of the other methods outlined in *Help! I'm a Parent!* But don't forget these principles of learning. They are really basic to all methods of discipline. Spankings, natural consequences, and communication will also fail if our children are still being rewarded for misbehavior.

ANSWER KEY TO EXERCISE I

1. a. By giving him a piece of candy when he cried.
   b. He will cry.
2. a. By thanking her (social reward) and by working on her dress (non-social reward).
   b. She will help with the dishes.
3. a. Attention
   b. Yes, by shouting which gave him the attention he was seeking.
   c. He will pester his sister.

4. a. By encouraging him and waiting for him to catch up.
   b. Keep walking and ignore him.
5. By imitation.

ANSWER KEY TO EXERCISE II-A

1. a. Confidence
   b. Power
   c. Love
   d. Attention
   e. Worth
   f. Perfection
   g. Revenge
   h. Psychological safety
2. Power was the main motivation. Revenge might also enter in.
3. Psychological safety was the main motivation. Attention might also enter in.
4. Psychological safety was the main motivation. Attention might also enter in, and she might be trying to get revenge by upsetting her parents with loud crying.

ANSWER KEY TO EXERCISE II-B

1. a. Giving in to her wishes.
   b. Becoming upset or spanking her and in that way giving more attention and satisfying her search for revenge.
   c. Consoling her by hugging and reassurance, thus rewarding her negative search for attention.
2. a. Hesitating to go out the door and giving her extra attention.
   b. Showing a sense of guilt over leaving and thus showing Marsha her manipulations are working.
   c. Promise Marsha not to go out so often.
   d. Promise to return home early.
3. a. Coming back into her room.
   b. Letting her stay up longer.
   c. Sleeping in bed with her.

ANSWER KEY TO EXERCISE II-D

1. a. Compliment her.
   b. Give her opportunities to make decisions in some matters.
   c. Listen to her opinions and show her respect.
   d. Take more time to play with her during the day.
   e. Get a baby-sitter she enjoys.
   f. Arrange something special for Marsha to do with the sitter.
   g. Play with her awhile each evening before she is put to bed.
   h. Encourage her to discuss any fears she has, such as being left alone in the dark.
   i. Take a few minutes to read a story, sing, pray, and/or talk after Marsha is in bed rather than putting her in bed and leaving immediately.

ANSWER KEY TO EXERCISE II-E

1. a. Stop giving in.
   b. Stop becoming upset and giving her reinforcement through attention and revenge.
   c. Stop giving her extra love or attention when she cries.
2. a. Stop hesitating when they leave.
   b. Stop promising not to go out as often.
   c. Stop showing a sense of guilt over leaving.
   d. Stop promising to return early.
3. a. Stop coming back into her room.
   b. Stop letting her stay up later.
   c. Stop sleeping with her.

ANSWER KEY TO EXERCISE II-F

1. a. The baby-sitter could give her a piece of candy or other desirable object.
   b. She could be allowed to watch an extra T.V. program.
   c. The sitter could read an extra story or plan an extra game.
   d. Her parents could bring her something upon returning home.
   e. Her parents could tell her she is a "big girl."
2. a. Give her an extra hug in the morning.
   b. Let her stay up five minutes longer (you will save more time than this when she stops crying!).
   c. Buy her something for her room.
   d. Tell her she is a "big girl."

Chapter 6

NATURAL AND LOGICAL CONSEQUENCES[1]

Most family conflicts involve a struggle for power between parent and child. Since the parent is stronger, he may be able to force his desires onto the child. But this rarely solves the problem. The power-hungry child fights back. He may not have his way, but at least he can make his parents miserable. This starts a vicious cycle. The child misbehaves. The parent tries to force him to conform. And the child fights back. Once this pattern is established, little peace remains. Every attempt at discipline degenerates into a struggle for power. This doesn't need to be. There are ways of extricating ourselves from battle so that we can calmly correct our children's misbehavior.

One of these ways is to use natural and logical consequences. By substituting natural and logical consequences for parental power and force, we can often discipline effectively without the usual hassle. Here are other important ideas for chapter five of *Help! I'm a Parent!*

- Although there is a definite place for the use of parental power and authority, we often overuse this power when disciplining children.
- Too much use of power and authority either smashes a child into

---

[1]This chapter is coordinated with "How Nature Disciplines Your Child," chapter five of *Help! I'm a Parent!*

neurotic submission or invites him to resist power by resorting to his own.

- We sometimes intervene in such areas as eating and getting up in the morning by nagging or trying to force children into desirable behavior. When we intervene like this, we are actually depriving children of opportunities to accept responsibility for their own behaviors.
- In natural consequences we simply let our children experience the natural results of their actions. After stepping on a hot sidewalk on a summer day, a child will remember to wear shoes the next time.
- The principle in logical consequences is similar to natural consequences. But in logical consequences nature doesn't have a built-in negative consequence. As parents, we select such a consequence and inform the child ahead of time. When he misbehaves, he suffers the logical consequence. We do not tell him, "I told you so," spank him, or motivate by guilt. Instead, he merely endures the promised consequence. A good logical consequence for being late to supper is to wait until the next meal to eat. A good consequence for not mowing the yard is to not play in the yard.
- When we are angry, logical consequences will not work. Our children sense that we are fighting to gain control of them rather than disciplining in a mature way.
- We often fail to use natural or logical consequences because of our own problems. We force children to do their homework or drive them to school after missing the bus because we are afraid they will fail. To help children mature, we must allow them to learn from the consequences of misbehavior.
- There are times to protect children and to intervene. We shouldn't let them suffer serious injury, for example. But we should allow children to endure some pain if it will teach a valuable lesson. Most of us are overly worried about our children's physical health and external performance. By focusing on these things, we often rear them incorrectly and cause long-term emotional suffering.
- Social isolation is an effective logical consequence. When a child is misbehaving, he can be calmly sent to his room. If this is done as a logical form of discipline, the child will profit from it. But if we send a child to his room because we are angry and want to punish him, we merely create more resentment.

EXERCISE I

When we sin, we often have a fear that God is going to intervene and severely punish us for our misbehavior. Although God does intervene and discipline, He often uses natural consequences instead. To get a better grasp of the concept of natural consequences, describe three occasions when you have misbehaved and God has let you suffer the natural consequences of your behavior to teach you a lesson.

1. ---

   ----

2. ---

   ----

3. ---

EXERCISE II

Here are several examples of parents who are learning to use natural and logical consequences. By studying the attitudes and methods these parents used, we can begin to see an effective way of applying logical consequences.

CHILDREN'S HOMEWORK

Mr. and Mrs. Ellis were worried over their son's schoolwork. Read the comments Mrs. Ellis makes and evaluate her success in avoiding a power struggle and applying natural consequences.

I have a problem with my Mark doing his homework. My husband has been helping him with his spelling and he is getting A's. But I found out this week that he was way down on his Iowa Test on spelling. The principal said he is either not retaining it or just wasn't in the mood that day and didn't try. That's the way he is. We thought we would try natural consequences; so we just left him alone. You said parents shouldn't nag about homework and that kids should handle their responsibility on their own. We tried it for several days, but he just got worse. It drove us crazy, because he just didn't care. Finally we said, "Well, do it whether you want to or not! And if it isn't done, you can't go with us Saturday!"

77

The Ellises attempted to apply natural consequences to help Mark take responsibility for his schoolwork. They were going to leave his work up to him and refuse to nag or coerce. This was the proper first step.

1. Did they follow through in their use of natural consequences?

   ----

2. Why do you think they failed to carry out their planned use of

   natural consequences? --

   ----

3. Natural and logical consequences will not work as long as we are using force on children. Whenever we use force, we risk perpetuating the power struggle. What did these parents do and

   say that proved they were still in a power struggle? -----------------

   ----

   ----

4. Why do you think this boy got even worse when his parents

   tried to apply natural consequences? -------------------------------

   ----

Let's summarize this attempt at discipline. Notice first that the Ellises were overly anxious. Mark was getting A's and the principal realized he may have just had a bad day on the Iowa Test. But the Ellises assumed the worst. They didn't give him credit for the A's or for a possible bad day. They expected him to do poorly.

It is evident that Mark's parents didn't fully understand natural consequences. They were still trying to force him to improve his spelling. Sensing this pressure, Mark got worse. He probably got this message from his parents: "We aren't happy with your Iowa tests and are upset because we've tried everything we know. In desperation we're going to quit bugging you for awhile. We think you will fail, but we will wait and see what happens." Mark sensed the frustration and lack of confidence in his parents' voice. He was tired of being pressured. He responded to their challenge by trying less. When this happened, Mark's parents were more upset. They threatened to punish him if he didn't get with it.

Here is what the Ellises could have done. They could have helped Mark with his spelling, but avoided pressuring him. They could have told him study was his responsibility and then stayed out of the struggle. When things got worse, they wouldn't get upset. The failure might be just the consequence Mark needed. If they were afraid to leave his performance to the natural consequence of poor grades, they could have structured a logical consequence. A good logical consequence for studying is no T.V. until the homework is done. Either of these ways would have avoided the power struggle and made Mark assume responsibility for his studies.

BEDWETTING[2]
Here is a completely successful application of logical consequences. Notice how these parents side-stepped a long-standing power struggle and made their son assume responsibility for his bedwetting.

> One thing has been driving me up the wall. Our boy is twelve and still wetting the bed. The doctor has tried medication and other things, but nothing works. There would be periods when he would be dry for a few days and then he'd do it every single night. It seems like he doesn't care at all. I was reading that a logical consequence would be to have him make his bed himself. I told him that if his bed was wet, he would change his sheets before he left for school. The first time it happened he said, "I'll never get it done." It was Saturday and he didn't change his sheets until eleven in the morning. I had to go off and by the time I got back it was done. The bed hasn't been wet since.

---

[2]In cases of persistent, regular bedwetting it is wise to consult a physician. If a physical disturbance is discovered it may not be wise to apply the logical consequence discussed here. In other cases, even with a seriously emotionally disturbed child, the logical consequence of changing his own sheets may still be basic to resolving the problem. Another means of solving the bedwetting problem is through the use of mechanical apparatuses. These instruments are constructed to set off a bell or administer a slightly painful, but harmless, electric shock as soon as any urine touches the bed sheet. This method is best reserved for cases when it is recommended by a professional person.

1. Of these eight basic motivations for human actions, which two were probably involved in this boy's bedwetting? ----------------------

----

2. The answer to the above question is attention and revenge. By having mother change his sheets, this boy got her attention daily. She showed her concern, talked to him, and took him to the doctor. All of these actions rewarded his bedwetting since they reinforced his attention-getting behavior. The bedwetting may also have been a sign of anger and revenge. He may have resented a younger sibling who was getting more attention. The bedwetting then served the dual purpose of gaining attention and punishing his mother for the attention he lost to his younger sister. If these were the dynamics, how would making him change his own sheets stop his bedwetting? ----------------------------------

----

ANSWER: It stopped rewarding both his attention-getting behavior and his attempts for revenge. Since his mother stopped giving extra attention, he lost that reason for bedwetting. Since he had to change his own sheets, he was no longer getting revenge on his mother. He was only hurting himself.

MESSY ROOMS

Here is another successful application of logical consequences. The Randalls were having difficulty motivating their two daughters to keep their room in order. They discussed the concept of responsibility and logical consequences with the girls. They explained that since Mrs. Randall needed help in the house, the daughters would be expected to clean their room. If anything was not in its place when the girls left for school, Mrs. Randall would pick it up and put it in a "Saturday Box." Since the item had been left out, it could not be retrieved until Saturday. In the past the Randalls had tried force, scoldings, and withdrawal of the girls' allowance. These methods had a mixed record of success and failure. Here is Mrs. Randall's summary of the first week's activity.

Monday:	"Room in order. Children eager to check box."
Tuesday:	"A few minor things in box."
Wednesday:	"Room orderly."
Thursday:	"Rita's new purse in the box. A few tears after school when she wanted it for tomorrow."
Friday:	"Room in order."
Saturday:	"Box cleaned out. Rita's sweat shirt in."

The logical consequence of a "Saturday Box" avoids the necessity of nagging and threatening and places the responsibility for a clean room where it belongs — on the child!

PICKING UP AFTER PLAY

Our neighbor boy comes over to play games quite often. In the hurry for him and Stan to go to dinner, picking up the game is often forgotten. This week I just mentioned that if the game were left, Harold would not be able to come over and play games. They both started picking it up immediately.

Here is another good example of using logical consequences with a common household problem. By quietly but firmly telling the children the consequences of failing to pick up after themselves, this mother saved herself a lot of work.

GETTING CHILDREN OFF TO SCHOOL

I've always had a real hassle getting Benny ready for school. It seems like I was constantly nagging and telling him to hurry. With two other children — oh boy! You've got three piles of homework to pick up and three sets of clothes to lay out. It seemed like I was constantly saying "Come do this! Come do that!" I was more rushed than they were, but I wasn't even going any place!

Thursday morning I told him once he'd better get ready or he was going to miss his ride. He just poked around and wasn't hurrying. He seemed to be getting slower and slower while my other kids kept getting ready. Pretty soon the horn honked. But Benny wasn't ready. He didn't have his shoes on and hadn't finished his cereal. I told the kids to go on and that Benny would have to stay home because he wasn't ready. He didn't think I was serious until he saw the kids go out the door and the car drive away. Then he jumped and screamed and said, "Why didn't you make them wait? You'll have to take me!" I said, "No, Benny. I want you to learn that you were late and didn't care about getting ready. You have to pay the penalty for that. You won't be able to go to school today."

Well, he really snapped to fast when he saw I meant business. He sat down and gobbled up his cereal and put on his shoes. The first thing he thought about was his perfect attendance. With a sad look on his face he said, "Now I won't get the card for not missing school, mom." That was enough for me. I melted. I felt, "How far do you go with a seven-year-old?" I knew we would both be disappointed at the end of the year, so I gave in. I said, "Well, I am going to Grandmother's, so I guess I can drop you off." I knew I should have carried it out but I couldn't. Anyway, it worked. The next morning he was a different boy. And he has been ever since.

Mrs. Briley was learning to apply logical consequences. She was tired of hassling her son each morning and decided to let him suffer the consequences of his dawdling. Basically, her attempt was a success. She taught her son to get ready on his own. This is a great release for every mother. But Mrs. Briley could have handled the situation better. She should have calmly told her son of her new plan the evening before, rather than waiting until she was upset. Mrs. Briley was actually still in a power struggle. She was frustrated and trying to punish Benny for his dawdling. Benny probably viewed her threat to let him miss his ride as a sign of his mother's frustration or as her attempt to punish him. If Mrs. Briley had discussed the problem calmly the night before, Benny would have known she was disciplining him for everyone's good rather than punishing him in a moment of frustration.

It would also have been better to carry out the consequence. Benny may have learned the lesson, "Mother really won't carry out her discipline if I can get her sympathy." This is one of our children's major ploys, and we shouldn't be manipulated by it.

WHEN BOYS CAN'T PLAY TOGETHER

My boys weren't playing well outside. One had used some ugly words; so I just brought him over and explained that we didn't like his behavior. I said, "I want you to stay in your room until you think you can play nicely. If you want to kick and yell, I'm going to move the clock back each time. The longer you yell, the longer you'll stay in your room."

I had to move it twice for Donald. He was in there twelve to fifteen minutes. He called me when he heard the bell ringing and said, "Mom, I'm sorry. I'll try to play nicer." I felt good about that. I didn't have to do anything except keep moving that clock! Twenty minutes later I did the same thing with Harvey. It didn't take him as long because he doesn't seem to be as rebellious as Donald. But it was about eight minutes.

I really felt the freedom of not being in a power struggle during those moments. Usually when I keep them in their room, I am arguing with them about what they did or didn't do.

This mother successfully applied logical consequences by using social isolation. If children cannot play together nicely, it is a logical consequence that they do not play at all. The key to social isolation is the parent's attitude. This mother had sent her sons to their rooms before and it hadn't worked. Apparently her own anger and frustration had caused the children to continue to argue and misbehave. When she decided to stop arguing and quietly carry out the consequence, her discipline began to work.

EXERCISE II

Now it's time to apply logical consequences to your children. On the next few pages there is a step-by-step plan to help you carry out a workable program of discipline through natural and logical consequences. Pick three different misbehaviors which are posing a problem in your family and which might be altered by using natural or logical consequences. Be sure to choose a specific problem such as throwing temper tantrums, being late for school, or failure to carry out the trash. If you choose an unspecific problem like "he's too messy" or "he isn't polite enough," you can't study that behavior and improve it. Behaviors must be specific.

FIRST MISBEHAVIOR

1. Describe the misbehavior --

----

2. Chart the frequency of the behavior for one week on the following graph. Do not begin to apply logical consequences until you have an accurate record of the frequency of the misbehavior.

```
       10 ┌───┬───┬───┬───┬───┬───┬───┐
        9 ├───┼───┼───┼───┼───┼───┼───┤
        8 ├───┼───┼───┼───┼───┼───┼───┤
NUMBER  7 ├───┼───┼───┼───┼───┼───┼───┤
 OF     6 ├───┼───┼───┼───┼───┼───┼───┤
MISBEHAVIORS 5 ├───┼───┼───┼───┼───┼───┼───┤
        4 ├───┼───┼───┼───┼───┼───┼───┤
        3 ├───┼───┼───┼───┼───┼───┼───┤
        2 ├───┼───┼───┼───┼───┼───┼───┤
        1 └───┴───┴───┴───┴───┴───┴───┘
          SUN  MON  TUES  WED  THUR  FRI  SAT
```

3. What method of discipline have you been using? ·················

···

4. What effect has your present method of discipline had? ········

···

5. What has been the emotional response of your child to your

present attempts at discipline? ··

···

6. What natural or logical consequence could you utilize to teach

your child better behavior? ···

···

7. Ask yourself the question, "Am I still angry or trying to force
my child into good behavior while we are in a power struggle?"

···

8. Ask yourself the question, "Is my choice of a consequence
really logically related to the misbehavior and did I set the

consequence calmly and for my child's good?" ····················

···

9. Have you taken time to communicate to your child your plan for logical consequences and the fact that it will be up to him to decide whether he is to do the desired thing or suffer the

consequence? ....

....

10. What was your child's response to the plan for logical

consequences? ....

....

11. Describe what happens the next time your child misbehaves. Include mention of your feelings in applying the logical consequence, your child's reaction and the success of the consequence. It usually takes a few applications of a consequence to change the behavior. Keep track of the number of misbehaviors on the following graph. Be sure that you consistently apply the consequence and avoid a power struggle.

....

....

....

....

		SUN	MON	TUES	WED	THUR	FRI	SAT
	10							
	9							
	8							
NUMBER	7							
OF	6							
MISBEHAVIORS	5							
	4							
	3							
	2							
	1							

SECOND MISBEHAVIOR

1. Describe the misbehavior -- -------

----

2. Chart the frequency of the behavior for one week on the following graph.

		SUN	MON	TUES	WED	THUR	FRI	SAT
	10							
	9							
	8							
NUMBER	7							
OF	6							
MISBEHAVIORS	5							
	4							
	3							
	2							
	1							

3. What method of discipline have you been using? ------------------

----

4. What effect has your present method of discipline had? --------

----

5. What has been the emotional response of your child to your

present attempts at discipline? --

----

6. What natural or logical consequence could you utilize to teach

your child better behavior? --

----

7. Ask yourself the question, "Am I still angry or trying to force my child into good behavior while we are in a power struggle?" --

8. Ask yourself the question, "Is my choice of a consequence really logically related to the misbehavior and did I set the consequence calmly and for my child's good?" -----------------------

9. Have you taken time to communicate to your child your plan for logical consequences and the fact that it will be up to him to decide whether he is to do the desired thing or suffer the consequence? --

    ----

10. What was your child's response to the plan for logical consequences? --

    ----

    ----

11. Describe what happens the next time your child misbehaves. Include mention of your feelings in applying the logical consequence, your child's reaction and the success of the consequence. It usually takes a few applications of a consequence to change the behavior. Keep track of the number of misbehaviors on the following graph. Be sure that you consistently apply the consequence and avoid a power struggle.

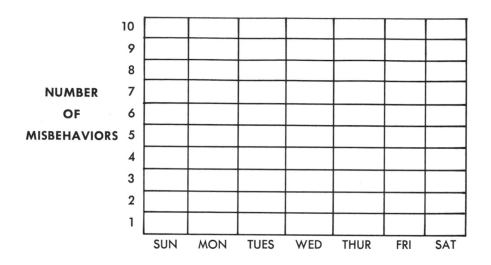

NUMBER
OF
MISBEHAVIORS

THIRD MISBEHAVIOR

1. Describe the misbehavior ---

----

2. Chart the frequency of the behavior for one week on the following graph.

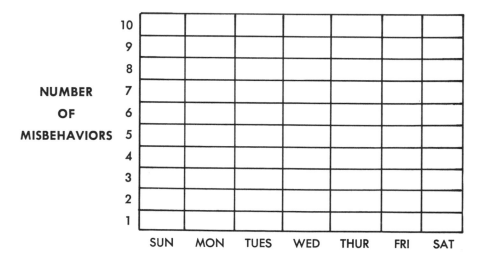

3. What method of discipline have you been using? --------------------

----

4. What effect has your present method of discipline had? --------

----

5. What has been the emotional response of your child to your

   present attempts at discipline? --

----

6. What natural or logical consequence could you utilize to teach

   your child better behavior? --

----

7. Ask yourself the question, "Am I still angry or trying to
   force my child into good behavior while we are in a power

   struggle?" --

8. Ask yourself the question, "Is my choice of a consequence
   really logically related to the misbehavior and did I set the

   consequence calmly and for my child's good?" --------------------

----

9. Have you taken time to communicate to your child your plan
   for logical consequences and the fact that it will be up to him
   to decide whether he is to do the desired thing or suffer the

   consequence? ---

----

10. What was your child's response to the plan for logical

consequences? --

----

11. Describe what happens the next time your child misbehaves. Include mention of your feelings in applying the logical consequence, your child's reaction and the success of the consequence. It usually takes a few applications of a consequence to change the behavior. Keep track of the number of misbehaviors on the following graph. Be sure that you consistently apply the consequence and avoid a power struggle.

	SUN	MON	TUES	WED	THUR	FRI	SAT
10							
9							
8							
7							
6							
5							
4							
3							
2							
1							

NUMBER OF MISBEHAVIORS

Chapter 7

THE USE OF PHYSICAL DISCIPLINE[1]

"Spare the rod and spoil the child" was a common quote before the 1940's. And in some circles the "good old fashioned whipping" is still in style. But during the last three decades many voices are rising up to protest "the abuses of corporal punishment." Spankings are seen to be either "inhuman," "sadistic," or "an expression of the parent's own problem." And in many cases this is true. Under the guise of discipline, many of us have wrongfully vented our anger on defenseless children. But does this mean we should give up spankings altogether? The answer is no. The Bible clearly teaches the necessity of physical spankings. Personal experience also tells us that they often work. But how do we know when and how to use this method? Here are a few suggestions from *Help! I'm a Parent!*

- Spanking is an important method of discipline, but it is only one of several ways of changing child behavior.
- Spanking should never be done in anger.
- Spankings should never be utilized when there is another effective method of discipline available.
- Spankings are usually more necessary in the first few years of life. After a child is old enough to communicate well and to profit from other measures, spanking should be ended.

---

[1]This chapter is coordinated with "To Spank or Not to Spank," chapter six of *Help! I'm a Parent!*

– Excessive use of physical discipline causes children to become fearful, depressed, or rebellious.
– Some parents refrain from spanking because of the overly severe punishment they received as children.

EXERCISE I

Make a record of the next three times you spank your child. Finish each of the spaces below to evaluate the effectiveness of your spankings.

1. Describe the first offense. --

    ----

    a. What was your emotional attitude when spanking your child? ---

       ----

       ----

    b. How hard and how often did you hit him? ----------------------

       ----

    c. What was your child's immediate emotional response? --------

       ----

    d. Was the spanking effective in changing the undesirable behavior? ---

    e. If the spanking didn't seem to be effective, there could be several reasons for its ineffectiveness: (1) there may have been a better method of discipline available, (2) you may have spanked in anger, (3) you may not have spanked hard enough, (4) you may be inconsistent, or (5) you may need to spank your child a few more times before he learns the lesson. Tell which of these reasons seem to have caused the failure of your spankings. -----------------------------------

----

----

2. Describe the second offense. --------------------------------------

----

----

a. What was your emotional attitude when spanking your child? ---

----

----

b. How hard and how often did you hit him? -------------------

----

c. What was your child's immediate emotional response? -------

----

d. Was the spanking effective in changing the undesirable behavior? --

e. If your spankings didn't work, what do you think caused their failures? --

----

----

3. Describe the third offense. --

----

  a. What was your emotional attitude when spanking your
     child? --

     ----

  b. How hard and how often did you hit him? -------------------

     ----

  c. What was your child's immediate emotional response? -------

     ----

  d. Was the spanking effective in changing the undesirable
     behavior? --

  e. If your spankings didn't work, what do you think caused
     their failures? --

Chapter 8

IMPROVING FAMILY COMMUNICATION[1]

Communication is probably the single most important element of discipline. Good communication is a deterrent to child misbehavior as well as a good corrective method. Here are five questions which can help you evaluate the quality of communication in your family. These questions reflect five basic principles of communication.

– Do I really want to listen?
– Can I show my child respect?
– Can I allow my children to express negative emotions without fear of retribution?
– Can I express an abundance of positive emotions?
– Am I open to new ideas and willing to admit I am wrong?

EXERCISE I

In each of the following examples of communication, list one or more of the five principles of communication which were violated and circle the number of the example which illustrates the best parental communication.[2]

---

[1]This chapter is coordinated with "Communication as a Method of Discipline," chapter seven of *Help! I'm a Parent!*
[2]See key at the end of this chapter for correct answers.

1. Child: "But I want to play a little longer."
   Parent: "I said no! Now, come in the house this minute!"

   a. Principles violated --

   ----

   b. Proper communication
      1. "Okay. You can stay out all night if you want to!"
      2. "I told you earlier you should hurry up or you wouldn't be finished."
      3. "You would really like to play a little longer, wouldn't you? Mother's sorry, but it's time to come in now. You can finish it tomorrow."

2. Mother: "I'll like you to wear your yellow dress to school today, Susie."

   Child: "Do I have to, Mother?"
   Mother: "Yes, that's what's best for you."

   a. Principles violated --

   ----

   b. Proper communication
      1. "I don't care. Wear anything you want."
      2. "What do you think would be nice, dear?"
      3. "Be sure and let mother know what you are wearing today, honey."

3. Child: "I hate you!"
   Parent: "Don't you talk to me like that!"

   a. Principles violated --

   ----

   b. Proper communication
      1. "I hate you, too!"
      2. "Go to your room and don't come out until I tell you!"

3. "That really made you mad, didn't it!"

4. Child: "I won't do it!"
   Parent (with a threatening voice): "Yes, you will!"

   a. Principles violated --

   ----

   b. Proper communication
      1. "Just wait till your father gets home!"
      2. "You really don't want to, do you?"
      3. "Okay. Forget it!"

5. Parent (angrily): "I've told you a hundred times not to play
   with that! Now look what you've done!"
   Child (fearfully): "I'm sorry."

   a. Principles violated --

   ----

   b. Proper communication
      1. (Calmly) "Those accidents happen, Scott. But mother
         has told you not to play in there. I'm going to have to
         spank you to help you learn to obey."
      2. "Come here this minute! Now pick up that mess and go
         to your room!"
      3. (Crying) "You've broken mother's vase. It's the only
         one I had. I can never replace it. I just don't know what
         I'll do. You've upset mother so!"

EXERCISE II (for wife)

To understand our children's feelings it is good to look at our own
reactions. In the spaces below describe two times when you have
experienced inadequate communication with your husband or a friend.

1. Description of the first poor communication ----------------------------

----

----

a. How did you feel toward yourself in response to this poor

communication? --

----

b. How did you feel toward the other person? ----------------------

----

c. What principles of communication were violated? --------------

----

d. What specific statements could you or the other person have
said which would have promoted better communication?

----

2. Description of the second poor communication ----------------------

----

----

a. How did you feel toward yourself in response to this poor

communciation? --

----

b. How did you feel toward the other person? --------------------

----

c. What principles of communication were violated? -------------

----

d. What specific statements could you or the other person have said which would have promoted better communication?

EXERCISE II (for husband)

In the spaces below, describe two times when you have experienced inadequate communication with your wife or a friend.

1. Description of the first poor communication --------------------

----

----

a. How did you feel toward yourself in response to this poor communication? --

----

b. How did you feel toward the other person? --------------------

----

c. What principles of communication were violated? ---------------

----

d. What specific statements could you or the other person have said which would have promoted better communication?

----

2. Description of the second poor communication -----------------------

----

----

a. How did you feel toward yourself in response to this poor communciation? ---

----

b. How did you feel toward the other person? -----------------------

----

c. What principles of communication were violated? ---------------

----

d. What specific statements could you or the other person have said which would have promoted better communication?

EXERCISE III

A. Select three instances of poor communication with your children. Analyze the dynamics of these inadequate communications by completing the following questions.

1. Describe the first poor communication. (Give exact quote if possible.) --

----

----

   a. What principles were violated? -------------------------------------

   ----

   ----

   b. How did your child respond to the poor communication?

   ----

   c. What was your tone of voice and attitude during the communication? --

   ----

   d. What could you have said that would have improved the communication? --

   ----

   ----

2. Describe the second poor communication. (Give exact quotes if possible.) --

----

----

   a. What principles were violated? -------------------------------------

      ----

      ----

   b. How did your child respond to the poor communication?

      ----

   c. What was your tone of voice and attitude during the communication? --

      ----

   d. What could you have said that would have improved the communication? --

      ----

      ----

3. Describe the third poor communication. (Give exact quote if possible.) ---

----

----

a. What principles were violated? ---------------------------

----

----

b. How did your child respond to the poor communication?

----

c. What was your tone of voice and attitude during the communication? ---

----

d. What could you have said that would have improved the communication? --

----

B. Select two potentially difficult times when you were able to promote healthy communication with your children.

1. Describe the first situation and quote what you said to promote good communication. --------------------------------

----

----

a. What was your tone of voice and attitude during the communication? ---

----

b. What principles did you follow which made the communication positive? ---

----

c. How did your child respond? ---

----

2. Describe the second situation and quote what you said to promote good communication. ---

----

----

a. What was your tone of voice and attitude during the communication? ---

----

b. What principles did you follow which made the communication positive? --

----

c. How did your child respond? --

ANSWER KEY FOR EXERCISE I

1. a. Can I show my child respect?
   b. 3
2. a. Do I really want to listen? Can I show my child respect?
   b. 2
3. a. Can I allow my children to express negative emotions without fear of retribution? Can I show my child respect?
   b. 3
4. a. Can I show my child respect? Can I allow my children to express negative emotions without fear of retribution?
   b. 2
5. a. Can I show my child respect? Can I express an abundance of positive emotions.
   b. 1

Chapter 9

SELECTING THE MOST EFFECTIVE
METHOD OF DISCIPLINE[1]

Now you have learned several ways of helping your children develop better patterns of behavior. These include spanking, communication, reinforcement, extinction, imitation, natural consequences, and logical consequences. There are times for each of these approaches. But no method is effective in every situation. The use of natural consequences helps us avoid the power struggle and the abuse of parental power. But exclusive reliance on this method fails to teach children submission to authority. On the other hand, although spankings often work, the overuse of this method can instill an unhealthy fear of all authority. The purpose of this chapter is to help you select the disciplinary method which is most appropriate to a specific problem setting. The following table summarizes the basic considerations in choosing a method of discipline.

---

[1]This chapter is coordinated with "Choosing the 'Right' Method of Discipline," chapter eight of *Help! I'm a Parent!*

TABLE 3

CHOOSING A METHOD OF DISCIPLINE

Method of Discipline	When to Use	Lesson the Child Learns
Communication	1. in all cases 2. before any other methods are tried	"By talking, I see the advantages and disadvantages of my planned action. Therefore, I will willingly do the proper thing. My parents respect me and I think they have good ideas."
Reinforcement	1. any time you want to strengthen a desirable behavior	"When I do the desirable thing, I get rewarded for it. Therefore, I will do it again."
Extinction	1. any time you want to weaken undesirable behavior	"When I behave undesirably, I do not get any reward. Therefore, there is no sense in doing that again."
Natural Consequences	1. when you want to weaken undesirable behavior 2. when communication and extinction have not worked	"When I do some things, I get hurt. Nobody else has anything to do with it. I just bring on a bad experience. Therefore, I will not do that again."
Logical Consequences	1. when you want to weaken undesirable behavior 2. when communication and extinction have not worked 3. when no natural consequence exists 4. when natural consequences would cause severe or lasting hurt to the child	"The world has many people. When I do something that is wrong, they may impose some undesirable consequences. Therefore, I will do my part in order to avoid the negative consequences."
Physical Spanking	1. when all other methods have failed	"My parents are my authority. They have the experience to know what is right and to enforce their guidelines by inflicting physical pain. Though I do not like it at the time, I am learning it is for my good and they do it because they love me."
Imitation	1. This method is in continuous operation.	"My parents are strong and grown-up. Since they act that way, so do I."

EXERCISE I

Circle the method of discipline most likely to be successful in the following examples.[2]

1. An eight-year-old who throws a temper tantrum
   a. Spanking
   b. Communication
   c. Imitation
   d. Extinction

2. A teenager who repeatedly breaks curfew
   a. Extinction
   b. Spanking
   c. Logical Consequences
   d. Reinforcement

3. A ten-month-old who purposely pours his drink onto the floor meal after meal
   a. Reinforcement
   b. Spanking
   c. Communication
   d. Extinction

4. A child who eats very little at meals and then keeps asking for snacks
   a. Spanking
   b. Reinforcement
   c. Natural Consequences
   d. Imitation

5. A four-year-old who repeatedly acts up while you are shopping
   a. Logical Consequences
   b. Spanking
   c. Reinforcement
   d. Natural Consequences

6. A sloppy child who won't pick up after himself
   a. Logical Consequences
   b. Spanking
   c. Imitation
   d. Nagging

---

[2]See key at the end of this chapter for correct answers.

7. An eleven-year-old "slow poke" who can't get going in the mornings
   a. Reinforcement
   b. Natural Consequences
   c. Imitation
   d. Extinction

8. A child who doesn't come when you call
   a. Reinforcement
   b. Logical Consequences
   c. Extinction
   d. Yelling Louder

9. A brother and sister fighting
   a. Spanking
   b. Natural Consequences
   c. Reinforcement
   d. Worrying

10. A three-year-old who disobeys
    a. Reinforcement
    b. Spanking
    c. Yelling
    d. Extinction

EXERCISE II

Spankings and natural and logical consequences are major ways of changing your child's behavior. To become sensitive to the appropriate applications of these methods, list all of the advantages and disadvantages you can think of for each method.[3]

1. Spankings

   a. Advantages --

---

[3]See key at the end of this chapter for answers to some of these questions.

b. Disadvantages --

----

2. Natural and logical consequences

  a. Advantages --

  ----

  b. Disadvantages ---

EXERCISE III

Effective discipline should accomplish several things. Of prime concern, of course, is to change a child's behavior. But beyond this are other tests of proper discipline. Here are five questions which help us understand the overall effect of our disciplinary measures.

- Did my child's behavior change?
- Did the discipline maintain my child's self-respect?
- Did the discipline give my child a proper image of loving authority?
- Were there any negative side effects of the discipline?
- Did the discipline promote a healthy relationship between my child and me?

Select three times you have recently disciplined your child. Using these guidelines, evaluate the effectiveness of your discipline and see if another method would have improved your results.

1. Describe the first misbehavior. --

----

a. How did you discipline? -----

----

b. Did your child's behavior change? ----- If not, why?

----

c. Did the discipline maintain your child's self-image? -----

In what way? -----

----

d. Did the discipline give your child a proper image of loving

authority? ----- In what way? -----

----

e. Were there any negative side effects? ----- If so, what

were they? -----

----

f. Did the discipline promote a healthy relationship between

you and your child? ----- In what way? -----

----

g. Do you now see another method that would be more

effective? ----- Which one? ----- How might

that method be more effective? -----

----

2. Describe the second misbehavior. ---

----

a. How did you discipline? --

----

b. Did your child's behavior change? ------------ If not, why?

----

c. Did the discipline maintain your child's self-image? ------------

In what way? --

----

d. Did the discipline give your child a proper image of loving

authority? ------------ In what way? ------------------------------------

----

e. Were there any negative side effects? ------------ If so, what

were they? ---

----

f. Did the discipline promote a healthy relationship between

you and your child? ------------ In what way? ------------------------

----

g. Do you now see another method that would be more

effective? ------------ Which one? --------------------------------------

How might that method be more effective? ------------------------

----

3. Describe the third misbehavior. -----------------------------

----

----

   a. How did you discipline? --------------------------------------

      ----

   b. Did your child's behavior change? ------------ If not, why?

      ----

   c. Did the discipline maintain your child's self-image? ------------

      In what way? ---

      ----

   d. Did the discipline give your child a proper image of loving

      authority? ------------ In what way? -----------------------------

      ----

   e. Were there any negative side effects? ------------ If so, what

      were they? --

      ----

   f. Did the discipline promote a healthy relationship between

      you and your child? ------------ In what way? -------------------

      ----

g. Do you now see another method that would be more effective? .... Which one? .... How might that method be more effective? ---

----

ANSWER KEY FOR EXERCISE I

1. d   6. a
2. c   7. b
3. b   8. b
4. c   9. b
5. a   10. b

ANSWER KEY FOR EXERCISE II

1. Spankings

Advantages:

Strong pain is a deterrent to misbehavior.
With very young children who cannot yet communicate verbally, spanking is often most easily understood.
Spankings are sometimes necessary with young children to demonstrate parental authority.

Disadvantages:

Spanking is often done in anger and this causes an unhealthy fear.
Excessive use of spanking promotes power struggles.
Excessive reliance on spanking teaches children to behave when the feared authority is present. But when the parental authority is not present, the child has no inner controls which would have been developed by the use of communication, natural consequences, reinforcement, and other methods.

2. Natural and Logical Consequences

Advantages:

Avoids the overuse of parental power and authority.
Teaches children to accept responsibility for their own behavior.
Avoids nagging, coercion or over-correction.

Disadvantages:

There are times when no effective consequence (except spanking) exists.
There are times for the loving but firm exercise of authority.

Chapter 10

BUILDING YOUR CHILD'S SELF-IMAGE[1]

Your child's self-image is the key to his adjustment. It determines the pattern of his entire personality. If we successfully build up our children's good feelings about themselves, they will be happy and well adjusted. If we don't, they will develop negative emotions of loneliness, anxiety, depression, and hostility. Three of the most important ingredients of a healthy self-esteem are: (1) a sense of belonging or a feeling of being loved, (2) a sense of worth or the feeling of being a good or valuable person, and (3) a sense of confidence in one's ability to perform.

As parents we are largely responsible for shaping our children's self-concepts. Here are several ways of building a positive self-esteem.

- Establish necessary rules in a fair and loving way.
- Discuss and explain the reasons for rules.
- Find substitute activities.
- Praise children frequently.
- Show respect.
- Avoid guilt motivations.
- Give responsibility.
- Promote individuality.

---

[1]This chapter is coordinated with chapters nine and ten of *Help! I'm a Parent!*

EXERCISE I

We need to become sensitive to our children's feelings about themselves. With very young children we do this by listening carefully to their verbal communication and observing their reactions. When our children are able to read and write, we can also get an indication of their self-esteem through sentence-completion tests and similar exercises. The next two exercises are designed to give you insights into your children's self-esteem. These exercises are not "psychological tests" and they do not show whether your child is "normal" or "abnormal." They are intended to give you a better idea of how he feels about himself. Some evening you may ask your children to "play some games with you." Ask them to fill out each of the exercises. If your child is over three years old, you can do these exercises even though he cannot read. Just tell him you want to play a game. Say, "This is a game. I am going to say some words and I want you to finish them." Give him a little help if necessary, but don't put words in his mouth. Write his answers down so you can study them later.

A. FIRST CHILD

1. My friends --

2. I wish --

3. When I play ---

4. School --

5. My mother ---

6. Most boys --

7. Sometimes I feel --

8. I have to ---

9. When I grow up --

10. Most girls --

11. I would live at some other house ---------------------------------

12. I get mad at --

13. I play alone ---

14. I worry about --

15. My brother --

16. If I were a parent, --

17. When I am spanked, --

18. Grown-ups ---

19. My sister --

20. Most boys and girls --

SECOND CHILD

1. My friends --

2. I wish --

3. When I play --

4. School --

5. My mother --

6. Most boys --

7. Sometimes I feel --

8. I have to ---

9. When I grow up ---

10. Most girls --

11. I would live at some other house ⸺⸺⸺⸺⸺⸺⸺

12. I get mad at ⸺⸺⸺⸺⸺⸺⸺⸺⸺⸺

13. I play alone ⸺⸺⸺⸺⸺⸺⸺⸺⸺⸺

14. I worry about ⸺⸺⸺⸺⸺⸺⸺⸺⸺

15. My brother ⸺⸺⸺⸺⸺⸺⸺⸺⸺⸺

16. If I were a parent, ⸺⸺⸺⸺⸺⸺⸺⸺

17. When I am spanked, ⸺⸺⸺⸺⸺⸺⸺

18. Grown-ups ⸺⸺⸺⸺⸺⸺⸺⸺⸺⸺

19. My sister ⸺⸺⸺⸺⸺⸺⸺⸺⸺⸺

20. Most boys and girls ⸺⸺⸺⸺⸺⸺⸺

THIRD CHILD

1. My friends ⸺⸺⸺⸺⸺⸺⸺⸺⸺⸺

2. I wish ⸺⸺⸺⸺⸺⸺⸺⸺⸺⸺⸺

3. When I play ⸺⸺⸺⸺⸺⸺⸺⸺⸺⸺

4. School ⸺⸺⸺⸺⸺⸺⸺⸺⸺⸺⸺

5. My mother ⸺⸺⸺⸺⸺⸺⸺⸺⸺⸺

6. Most boys ⸺⸺⸺⸺⸺⸺⸺⸺⸺⸺

7. Sometimes I feel ⸺⸺⸺⸺⸺⸺⸺⸺

8. I have to ⸺⸺⸺⸺⸺⸺⸺⸺⸺⸺

9. When I grow up ⸺⸺⸺⸺⸺⸺⸺⸺

10. Most girls ⸺⸺⸺⸺⸺⸺⸺⸺⸺⸺

11. I would live at some other house --

12. I get mad at --

13. I play alone --

14. I worry about ---

15. My brother --

16. If I were a parent, --

17. When I am spanked, --

18. Grown-ups ---

19. My sister --

20. Most boys and girls --

B. FIRST CHILD

Answer each of these questions:

1. If you had a wish and your wish would come true, what would

   you wish? ---

   ----

2. What would you do if you had a hundred dollars? -----------------

   ----

3. What do you want to be when you grow up? ------------------------

   ----

4. What is the best thing that ever happened to you? ----------------

   ----

5. What is the worst thing that ever happened to you? ----------------

----

6. Would you rather be a boy or a girl? -------------------------------

7. Tell three things you like best about yourself. --------------------

----

----

8. Tell three things you don't like about yourself. -------------------

----

----

9. If you could be changed and be different from what you are, how would you want to be changed? ----------------------------

----

10. If you could be anybody you wanted to be, who would you most like to be? --

SECOND CHILD

Answer each of these questions:

1. If you had a wish and your wish would come true, what would you wish? --

----

2. What would you do if you had a hundred dollars? ----------------

----

3. What do you want to be when you grow up? ----------------------------

----

4. What is the best thing that ever happened to you? -----------------

----

5. What is the worst thing that ever happened to you? -------------

----

6. Would you rather be a boy or a girl? ----------------------------------

7. Tell three things you like best about yourself. ----------------------

----

----

8. Tell three things you don't like about yourself. ---------------------

----

----

9. If you could be changed and be different from what you are,

   how would you want to be changed? -----------------------------------

----

10. If you could be anybody you wanted to be, who would you

    most like to be? --

THIRD CHILD

Answer each of these questions:

1. If you had a wish and your wish would come true, what

would you wish? --

----

2. What would you do if you had a hundred dollars? ----------------

----

3. What do you want to be when you grow up? ----------------

----

4. What is the best thing that ever happened to you? ----------------

----

5. What is the worst thing that ever happened to you? ----------------

----

6. Would you rather be a boy or a girl? ----------------------------------

7. Tell three things you like best about yourself. ----------------------

----

----

8. Tell three things you don't like about yourself. ----------------------

----

----

9. If you could be changed and be different from what you are,

how would you want to be changed? ----------------------------

----

10. If you could be anybody you wanted to be, who would you

most like to be? --

C. The questions and sentence completions your child filled out should tell a lot about his self-image. By studying his answers you can see many of his feelings. You can see what negative feelings bother him and the things he likes and dislikes about himself. Make a list of several negative feelings which showed up in his answers.

FIRST CHILD

1. _____

2. _____

3. _____

4. _____

5. _____

SECOND CHILD

1. _____

2. _____

3. _____

4. _____

5. _____

THIRD CHILD

1. _____

2. _____

3. _____

4. _____

5. _____

D. What can you do to help your child overcome these feelings and develop a healthy self-image?

FIRST CHILD

1. --

2. --

3. --

4. --

5. --

SECOND CHILD

1. --

2. --

3. --

4. --

5. --

THIRD CHILD

1. --

2. --

3. --

4. --

5. --

EXERCISE II

A. For one day give careful attention to experiences which influence your child's self-image. Keep track of each time you make one of the following types of reactions:

- Criticism
- Praise
- Telling child to stop an activity
- Suggesting an interesting activity a child can do

Place a check mark in the table each time you make one of these reactions.

CHILD ONE

	1	2	3	4	5	6	7	8	9	10
Criticism										
Praise										
Telling to Stop										
Suggesting Alternatives										

CHILD TWO

	1	2	3	4	5	6	7	8	9	10
Criticism										
Praise										
Telling to Stop										
Suggesting Alternatives										

CHILD THREE

	1	2	3	4	5	6	7	8	9	10
Criticism										
Praise										
Telling to Stop										
Suggesting Alternatives										

B. After studying your typical reactions and noting actions which may tear at your child's self-image, plot your behavior again. See if you can substitute ego-building reactions for potentially destructive ones.

CHILD ONE

	1	2	3	4	5	6	7	8	9	10
Criticism										
Praise										
Telling to Stop										
Suggesting Alternatives										

CHILD TWO

	1	2	3	4	5	6	7	8	9	10
Criticism										
Praise										
Telling to Stop										
Suggesting Alternatives										

CHILD THREE

	1	2	3	4	5	6	7	8	9	10
Criticism										
Praise										
Telling to Stop										
Suggesting Alternatives										

EXERCISE III

Rules and parental guidance are important to a child's safety and security. But they should be employed only when necessary and then with good reason. Here are a few important reasons for rules and parental guidance.

- Protect your child's physical safety.
- Promote order and mutual respect in the family and other social situations.
- Teach biblical standards.
- Give children a sense of security by setting limits on the impulsive acting out of impulses or carnal actions.

Some of us overprotect our children or set too many rigid rules. We do this with good intentions, but the effect is just the same. We need to become sensitive to the reasons why we set too many regulations. Here are a few:

- A fear that physical or spiritual harm will come to children if we don't protect them. This doesn't let children learn from their mistakes.

– A personality rigidity. We are often set in our ways and unable to be sensitive to our children's needs.
– A carry-over from our parents' overly strong or rigid controls. Since we were reared in a firm, authoritarian home, we think this is the proper way of doing things.
– A genuine concern to train our children spiritually coupled with the mistaken belief that control and regulation are the primary ways of teaching Christian character. This view neglects the prime importance of deep communication and sensitivity to our children's needs.
– A distorted, legalistic view of Christianity which overemphasizes external behavior at the expense of a biblical emphasis on warmth, unconditional acceptance and inner peace.
– Hostility and frustrations which cause us to overreact and set limits or punish because we are upset rather than because our children are in need of discipline.

With your husband or wife, make a list of five rules and regulations you usually apply to your children. Think each reason through carefully and tell what purpose the rule is serving or what need it is meeting. If the rule seems to be unnecessary, tell what you think caused you to establish it. Also, give your children's reaction to each rule and tell if you and your mate agree on your regulations.

1. Rule One ⸻⸻⸻⸻⸻⸻⸻⸻⸻⸻

    ⸻⸻⸻⸻⸻⸻⸻⸻⸻⸻

    a. Purpose of the rule ⸻⸻⸻⸻⸻⸻⸻⸻

        ⸻⸻⸻⸻⸻⸻⸻⸻⸻⸻

        ⸻⸻⸻⸻⸻⸻⸻⸻⸻⸻

    b. Explanation for rule if unnecessary ⸻⸻⸻⸻

        ⸻⸻⸻⸻⸻⸻⸻⸻⸻⸻

        ⸻⸻⸻⸻⸻⸻⸻⸻⸻⸻

c. Child's reaction --

----

d. Do you and your mate agree on the rule? ---------------------

----

2. Rule Two --

----

   a. Purpose of the rule --

----

   b. Explanation of rule if unnecessary ----------------------------

----

----

   c. Child's reaction --

----

   d. Do you and your mate agree on the rule? ---------------------

----

3. Rule Three --

----

   a. Purpose of the rule --

----

b. Explanation for rule if unnecessary ----------------------------------

----

----

c. Child's reaction --

----

d. Do you and your mate agree on the rule? ------------------------

----

4. Rule Four --

----

a. Purpose of the rule --

----

b. Explanation for rule if unnecessary ----------------------------

----

----

c. Child's reaction --

----

d. Do you and your mate agree on the rule? ----------------------------

----

5. Rule Five --

----

   a. Purpose of the rule ---

----

   b. Explanation for rule if unnecessary ---------------------------

----

----

   c. Child's reaction --

----

   d. Do you and your mate agree on the rule? ----------------------

----

EXERCISE IV

A sense of individuality and confidence in his abilities is vital to a child's self-image. For a three-day period of Friday, Saturday, and Sunday, try to be especially sensitive to your child's sense of individuality and self-confidence. Make a list of things you do or say which might subtly tear at this part of his self-esteem. This includes criticism, ridicule, overprotection, unnecessary rules, or a subtle impression that "You are only a child. Better let mother and dad do that!"

   1. Experiences which hinder a child's development of a sense of confidence and individuality.

130

----

2. Experiences which strengthen your child's sense of confidence and individuality.

EXERCISE V

When your child is depressed, he is usually feeling like a failure, unworthy, or lonely. Pick one time of depression for each of your children and discuss it below.

FIRST CHILD

1. Describe his looks and feelings during this time of depression.

----

2. What do you think caused the depression? ----------------------

----

----

3. Which self-concept needs are probably not being met and

causing the depression? --

----

4. What can you do in a similar situation to help him out of the

depression? --

----

5. What could you have done to prevent the depression? ------------

----

SECOND CHILD

1. Describe his looks and feelings during this time of depression.

----

2. What do you think caused the depression? ------------------------------

----

----

3. Which self-concept needs are probably not being met and

causing the depression? --

----

4. What can you do in a similar situation to help him out of the

depression? --

----

5. What could you have done to prevent the depression? -------------

----

THIRD CHILD

1. Describe his looks and feelings during this time of depression.

----

2. What do you think caused the depression? -------------------------

----

----

3. Which self-concept needs are probably not being met and

causing the depression? --

----

4. What can you do in a similar situation to help him out of the

depression? --

----

5. What could you have done to prevent the depression? -------------

----

Chapter 11

HOW TO HANDLE HOSTILITY[1]

No discipline is truly effective when we are angry. Although we may get the desired external behavior by frightening children with our tempers, this actually causes serious inner problems. Children respond to our hostility by fearful obedience, outward retaliation, or pent-up anger. None of these reactions are healthy. To discipline effectively, we must learn to handle our feelings of anger and frustration. The major points in chapter eleven of *Help! I'm a Parent!* are listed below.

– Hostility is a destructive emotion for both the parent and child.
– The Bible describes hostility as sin (James 1:19-21 and Galatians 5:19-21).
– Righteous indignation differs from carnal hostility in that it (a) always coexists with love, (b) is never used selfishly to gain revenge or defend oneself, and (c) comes from a desire for righteousness.
– Hostility can be resolved as we mature and become sensitive to our feelings. The important steps in overcoming anger include:

1. Becoming aware of our subtle feelings of anger and frustration.
2. Understanding the causes of our hostility.

---

[1]This chapter is coordinated with "Losing Your Cool," chapter eleven of *Help! I'm a Parent!*

3. Realizing that there are no "accidents" with God and that even potentially frustrating experiences can be faced happily if we are willing to learn from them.
4. Thanking God for the lessons we can learn from frustrating events.

EXERCISE I (for wife)

To see the strong effect of hostility on our children, we need to take a look at ourselves. In the spaces below discuss two times when you were the recipient of someone else's hostility. Choose the strongest anger you can remember receiving from one of your parents and from your husband.

1. Describe the anger directed toward you by your parent. ....

----

    a. What had you done to precipitate the anger? ....

    ----

    b. Why do you think your parent was so upset? ....

    ----

    c. How did you feel about yourself after the outburst? ....

    ----

    d. How did you feel toward your parent? ....

    ----

2. Describe the anger directed toward you by your husband. ......

----

   a. What had you done to precipitate the anger? ....

     ----

   b. Why do you think your husband was so upset? ....

     ----

   c. How did you feel about yourself after the outburst? ....

     --   ---------------

     ----

   d. How did you feel toward your husband? ----------------------

     ----

EXERCISE I (for husband)

Choose the strongest anger you can remember receiving from one of your parents and from your wife.

   1. Describe the anger directed toward you by your parent. ....

     ----

   a. What had you done to precipitate the anger? ....

     ----

b. Why do you think your parent was so upset? ----------------------

----

c. How did you feel about yourself after the outburst? ------------

----

----

d. How did you feel toward your parent? -------------------------------

----

----

2. Describe the anger directed toward you by your wife. ------------

----

----

a. What had you done to precipitate the anger? ----------------------

----

b. Why do you think your wife was so upset? -------------------------

----

c. How did you feel about yourself after the outburst? ------------

----

----

d. How did you feel toward your wife? --------------------------------

----

EXERCISE II (for wife)

Choose two times when you have been angry at your children and analyze them below.

1. Describe the first instance of your anger. ---------------------------------

   ----

   ----

   a. What did your child do that made you mad? ---------------------------

      ----

   b. Why did that upset you so? --

      ----

   c. How did your child react to your anger? ---------------------------

      ----

      ----

   d. How do you think he felt after receiving your anger? ----------

      ----

      ----

   e. What good came out of your anger? ----------------------------------

      ----

   f. If any good came out of your anger, do you think it offsets

      the negative feelings it set off in your child? ----------------------

      ----

g. What do you think God was trying to teach you by allowing your child to misbehave and tempt you to lose your

temper? --

----

2. Describe the second instance of your anger. ----------------------------

----

----

a. What did your child do that made you mad? ---------------------

----

b. Why did that upset you so? ---------------------------------------

----

c. How did your child react to your anger? ----------------------

----

----

d. How do you think he felt after receiving your anger? ---------

----

----

e. What good came out of your anger? ----------------------------

----

f. If any good came out of your anger, do you think it offsets

the negative feelings it set off in your child? ----------------------

----

g. What do you think God was trying to teach you by allow-ing your child to misbehave and tempt you to lose your temper? ....

....

If you would really like to change, ask God to make you sensitive to your anger, to show you what caused it, and to help you understand what He is trying to teach you through frustrating circumstances. In short, start learning to thank God for instances of your child's mis-behavior since they are ways of conforming you into the image of Christ. As with all strong emotions, hostility cannot be resolved over-night. These principles are intended to give you a start on resolving your hostility. The actual process may take months or even years.

EXERCISE II (for husband)

Choose two times when you have been angry at your children and analyze them below.

1. Describe the first instance of your anger. ....

....

....

   a. What did your child do that made you mad? ....

   ....

   b. Why did that upset you so? ....

   ....

   c. How did your child react to your anger? ....

   ....

   d. How do you think he felt after receiving your anger? ....

----

e. What good came out of your anger? ---------------------------------

----

f. If any good came out of your anger, do you think it offsets the negative feelings it set off in your child? ---------------------

----

g. What do you think God was trying to teach you by allow-ing your child to misbehave and tempt you to lose your temper? ---

----

2. Describe the second instance of your anger. ---------------------------

----

----

a. What did your child do that made you mad? ---------------------

----

b. Why did that upset you so? ---------------------------------------

----

c. How did your child react to your anger? ---------------------------

----

----

d. How do you think he felt after receiving your anger? ----------

----

----

e. What good came out of your anger? ------------------------------------

----

f. If any good came out of your anger, do you think it offsets

   the negative feeling it set off in your child? ------------------------------

----

g. What do you think God was trying to teach you by allowing your child to misbehave and tempt you to lose your

   temper? --

If you would really like to change, ask God to make you sensitive to your anger, to show you what caused it, and to help you understand what He is trying to teach you through frustrating circumstances. In short, start learning to thank God for instances of your child's misbehavior since they are ways of conforming you into the image of Christ. As with all strong emotions, hostility cannot be resolved overnight. These principles are intended to give you a start on resolving your hostility. The actual process may take months or even years.

Chapter 12

OVERCOMING GUILT[1]

Children often con us into doing their work or failing to carry out needed discipline by playing on our consciences. By making us feel, "I guess I'm being a little firm" or, "I sure hate to see him suffer that way," they get us where they want us. Not being able to tolerate the guilty feeling, we soon give in. Through this mechanism, many children trick us into doing their homework. Others avoid physical spankings by playing on our sympathy. In either case, we are refraining from proper methods of child training because of our overly sensitive consciences.

EXERCISE I (for wife)

To become sensitive to how children manipulate us, discuss two times when you have manipulated others through guilt. You may remember times with your parents, your friends, your husband, or your children. The following questions will help you analyze this problem.

    1. Describe the first instance in which you motivated someone by

        guilt. --

---

[1]This chapter is coordinated with "Guilt: Your Child's Best Weapon," chapter twelve of *Help! I'm a Parent!*

143

----

a. As near as you can recall, what were your exact words?

----

b. Why do you think you used this method of motivation?

----

c. How did the other person respond? --

----

d. How do you think the other person felt? --

----

e. How did you feel after you manipulated the other person

through guilt? --

----

f. What would have been a more mature and honest method

of motivation? --

----

2. Describe the second time when you motivated someone by

guilt. --

----

a. As near as you can recall, what were your exact words?

----

b. Why do you think you used this method of motivation?

----

c. How did the other person respond? ---

----

d. How do you think the other person felt? ---

----

e. How did you feel after you manipulated the other person through guilt? ---

----

f. What would have been a more mature and honest method of motivation? ---

----

EXERCISE I (for husband)

To become sensitive to how children manipulate us, discuss two times when you have manipulated others through guilt. You may remember times with your parents, your friends, your wife, or your children. The following questions will help you analyze this problem.

1. Describe the first instance in which you motivated someone by guilt. --

----

----

   a. As near as you can recall, what were your exact words?

   ----

   b. Why do you think you used this method of motivation?

   ----

   c. How did the other person respond? ----------------------------

   ----

   d. How do you think the other person felt? --------------------

   ----

   ----

   e. How did you feel after you manipulated the other person through guilt? --

   ----

   f. What would have been a more mature and honest method

of motivation? --

----

2. Describe the second time when you motivated someone by

    guilt. --

    ----

    a. As near as you can recall, what were your exact words?

        ----

    b. Why do you think you used this method of motivation?

        ----

    c. How did the other person respond? ----------------------------------

        ----

    d. How do you think the other person felt? ----------------------------

        ----

        ----

    e. How did you feel after you manipulated the other person

        through guilt? --

        ----

    f. What would have been a more mature and honest method

of motivation? ....

....

EXERCISE II

Select two times when your children have motivated you by guilt. Answer the questions below to gain further insight into this dynamic.

1. Describe the first example of your child using guilt to manipu-

   late you. ....

   ....

   ....

   a. What was he trying to get you to do by making you feel

      guilty? ....

   b. How did you feel when he tried to manipulate your

      feelings? ....

      ....

   c. Did you give in and take over some of his responsibilities

      or let him escape some deserved consequence? ....

      ....

   d. What in your background has made you sensitive to this

      type of manipulation? ....

      ....

   e. How could you have responded to this manipulation? ....

----

2. Describe the second time your child used guilt to manipulate you. --

----

----

  a. What was he trying to get you to do by making you feel guilty? --

  b. How did you feel when he tried to manipulate your feelings? --

  ----

  c. Did you give in and take over some of his responsibilities or let him escape some deserved consequence? ----------------

  ----

  d. What in your background has made you sensitive to this type of manipulation? --

  ----

  e. How could you have responded to this manipulation? -------

  ----

Chapter 13

WORRY IS A WEAPON [1]

Worry is a major cause of parental mistakes. Most of us "know" how to treat our children. But our own fears often impel us to intervene where we don't belong. The major ideas of this chapter are:

- Whenever possible, we should refuse to let children manipulate us into intervening in their affairs. This applies to eating and fighting as well as many other areas where children will solve their own problems if we stay out of the way.
- When our anxiety motivates us to intervene where we don't belong, we rob children of a chance to develop personal responsibility.
- Although we should "protect" our children from severe physical harm, we should let them suffer many of the less severe consequences of misbehavior. Physical pain can teach lessons with a lasting value much more effectively than most other methods.
- Children often play on our tendency to worry to get us involved in a power struggle, to seek increased attention, or to get us to take sides in their disputes.
- The best way to resolve sibling conflicts is to stay out of the way and let them work out their own problems.
- The next most effective way to resolve sibling conflicts is to use the logical consequence of social isolation. Children can be told,

---

[1]This chapter is coordinated with "Fear: the Enemy of Peaceful Parenthood," chapter thirteen of *Help! I'm a Parent!*

"If you cannot play together nicely, you will each have to go to your room." Although it is usually better to let children solve their own fights, social isolation is certainly preferable to other methods.

EXERCISE I

Circle the most appropriate response to the following childish attempts to motivate you by fear.[2]

1. Tim, your seven-year-old, says his older brother Bill is "picking on" him.
   a. "Cut it out, Bill! I've told you to quit pestering Tim!"
   b. "If you'd leave him alone, Tim, Bill would probably stop pestering you."
   c. "I'm sure you boys can work out your own differences."

2. At eight in the evening your ten-year-old daughter says, "Mother, you've got to help with this report. If I don't get it in tomorrow, I can't get a B."
   a. "I'm sorry, Mary, I could have helped you, but I can't at the last minute."
   b. "I've told you not to put things off like this. Now hurry up and let's get it done. But remember, this is the last time!"
   c. "I've told you not to put things off. Maybe this will teach you a lesson. I hope you get a C."

3. Your nine-year-old dawdles every morning. One morning after getting up late and slowly getting ready, she says, "Mother! Find my books and bring my lunch, quick. I'm going to miss the bus."
   a. "Okay. Here are your books. Quick, out the door!"
   b. "Get them yourself. It's about time you grew up!"
   c. "I'm sorry, dear. Mom's busy with her work. You can get your books."

4. Your child throws a temper tantrum, kicks his feet, and bangs his head on the floor.
   a. "Stop that this minute!"
   b. "All right, Billy. Go ahead and do what you want."
   c. Ignore him completely or say, "If you want to do that you may, but it won't help you get your way."

---

[2]See key at the end of this chapter for correct answers.

5. Your daughter threatens, "If you won't let me go, I'll scream!"
   a. "If you do, I'll tan your hide."
   b. "You may scream if you like, Janice, but you still cannot go."
   c. "Please don't, Janice. Please do what Mother asks."

EXERCISE II

List three times you have unnecessarily intervened in your child's activities. Try to gain some insight into your reactions by answering the following questions.

1. Describe the first behavior which caused you to intervene. --------

   ----

   ----

   a. What were you feeling as you observed your child in that

      behavior? --

      ----

   b. What do you think caused you to feel that way? ---------------

      ----

      ----

   c. How did your child respond when you intervened? -------------

      ----

   d. Did your intervention build up his self-esteem? ----------------

      In what way? --

      ----

   e. What would your child have learned if you had not

intervened? --

----

2. Describe the second behavior which caused you to intervene.

----

    a. What were you feeling as you observed your child in that

       behavior? --

       ----

    b. What do you think caused you to feel that way? ----------------

       ----

       ----

    c. How did your child respond when you intervened? ----------

       ----

    d. Did your intervention build up his self-esteem? ----------------

       In what way? --

       ----

    e. What would your child have learned if you had not

       intervened? --

       ----

3. Describe the third behavior which caused you to intervene.

----

a. What were you feeling as you observed your child in that behavior? --

----

b. What do you think caused you to feel that way? --------------

----

c. How did your child respond when you intervened? -----------

----

d. Did your intervention build up his self-esteem? --------------

In what way? ---

----

e. What would your child have learned if you had not intervened? --

----

ANSWER KEY FOR EXERCISE I

1. c
2. a
3. c
4. c
5. b

Chapter 14

A PERSPECTIVE FOR CHANGE

Now you have finished a complete program designed to improve your relations with your children. This final chapter will help review your progress and plan for future growth.

EXERCISE I

A. Looking back over the insights you have attempted to apply, list the specific changes you have seen in your attitudes and actions since beginning this program.

1. ---

2. ---

3. ---

4. ---

5. ---

B. What changes have you seen in your children's behavior?

FIRST CHILD

1. ---

2. ---

3. ---

4. ---

5. ---

SECOND CHILD

1. ---

2. ---

3. ---

4. ---

5. ---

THIRD CHILD

1. ---

2. ---

3. ---

4. ---

5. ---

EXERCISE II

A. To evaluate the present status of your child's adjustment, make a list of all the positive actions and attitudes each of your children display.

FIRST CHILD

1. ---

2. ---

3. --

4. --

5. --

6. --

7. --

8. --

SECOND CHILD

1. --

2. --

3. --

4. --

5. --

6. --

7. --

8. --

THIRD CHILD

1. --

2. --

3. --

4. --

5. --

6. --

7. --

8. --

B. List negative attitudes and actions which still need to be improved.

FIRST CHILD

1. --

2. --

3. --

4. --

5. --

6. --

7. --

8. --

SECOND CHILD

1. --

2. --

3. --

4. --

5. --

6. --

7. ---

8. ---

THIRD CHILD

1. ---

2. ---

3. ---

4. ---

5. ---

6. ---

7. ---

8. ---

A FINAL WORD

Raising children is a big task and all good parents are in a process of growth. The readings and exercises you have completed have helped you learn new and effective ways of working with children. But they are only a beginning. The process of parenthood draws on our total resources. Our complete character will be reflected in our children. Because of this, no book or set of techniques can turn us into "instant parents." My sincere desire is that each of us will maintain an open attitude toward spiritual and emotional growth. Only as we are in a process of growing into the maturity of Christ's character can we really become "effective parents." Then we can really "train up our children in the way they should go" and have the assurance that "when they grow old they will not depart from it."

BEHAVIOR CHARTS

Name of Child................................ Behavior................................

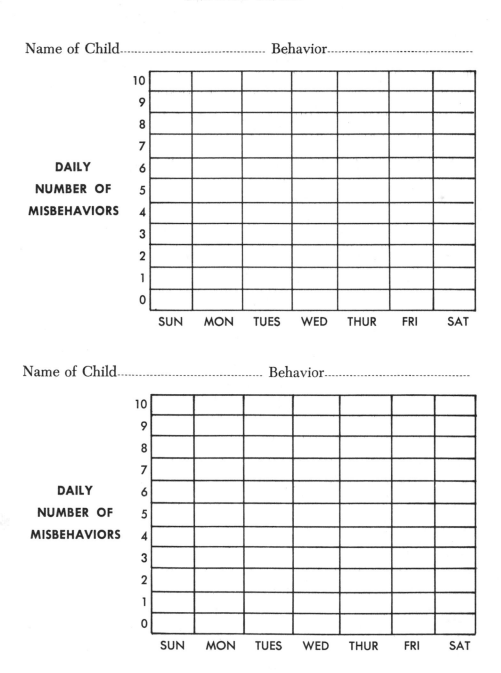